"With this book, you are accompanied by your personal story-telling guide while discovering this underappreciated region of North America. Wisdom on geology, natural history emphasizing birds, wildlife management, and history is offered in an engaging narrative."
—Gary C. White, professor emeritus of fish, wildlife, and conservation biology at Colorado State University

"This book entices and prepares readers to make their own personal connection to the heart of North America through its most inspiring occupants, Great Plains birds."
—Sarah Sortum, rancher and ecotourism provider

"From modern day prairie birds (and where to see them), to geography, history, and conservation, this book is an excellent introduction for anyone wanting to learn more about the vast heart of America, the Great Plains. Wonders abound, if only we look."
—Joel Sartore, Photo Ark founder and *National Geographic* photographer and fellow

"My high expectations were met when I read Larkin's book *Great Plains Birds*, but they were exceeded when I found myself laughing and living vicariously through his personal narrative. This book is honest and important and presents a clear-eyed view of bird conservation today in our heartland."
—Michael Forsberg, photographer and author of *Great Plains: America's Lingering Wild*

T0324289

GREAT

DISCOVER THE GREAT PLAINS

Series Editor: Richard Edwards, Center for Great Plains Studies

LARKIN POWELL

PLAINS
Birds

UNIVERSITY OF NEBRASKA PRESS   *Lincoln*

A Project of the Center for Great Plains Studies, University of Nebraska

Library of Congress Cataloging-
in-Publication Data
Names: Powell, Larkin A., author.
Title: Great Plains birds / Larkin Powell.
Description: Lincoln: University of
Nebraska Press, [2019] | Series: Discover
the Great Plains | Includes index.
Identifiers: LCCN 2019006780
ISBN 9781496204189 (paperback: alk. paper)
ISBN 9781496218599 (epub)
ISBN 9781496218605 (mobi)
ISBN 9781496218612 (pdf)
Subjects: LCSH: Birds—Great Plains. |
Birds—Great Plains—Pictorial works.
Classification: LCC QL683.G68 P69 2019 |
DDC 598.09764/8—dc23 LC record available
at https://lccn.loc.gov/2019006780

Set in Garamond Premier by Mikala R. Kolander.
Designed by N. Putens.

To my teachers: Lyle Babberl, Charles Eilers, and Nicholas Hartwig, who inspired my passion for nature, and John Judd, James Lippold, Lana Hicks, and Jon Wallace, who showed me how to tell stories

A wild turkey on the Great Plains, from W. E. Webb, *Buffalo Land* (1872).

All rivers and creeks were alive with beaver, otter, mink, muskrats and raccoons, along with various kinds of geese, ducks, pelicans, swans, and other water birds. These birds of passage appeared by the thousands every spring and fall. Cranes, gray and white, and several species of wood cocks were seen in large flocks. All this had changed entirely in the fifty years that have passed since the founding of our settlement. The above-mentioned birds and animals whose great multitudes gave the land its peculiar character and appeal in those early days have decreased in numbers to almost the vanishing point.

—William Stolley, 1907

CONTENTS

ILLUSTRATIONS

ACKNOWLEDGMENTS

I am grateful to anyone who has shared time in the woods, wetlands, or grasslands during birding and research adventures with me, because shared moments are sacred moments. Eventually stories seem to come from sacred moments.

Richard C. (Rick) Edwards challenged me with this project and Katie Nieland provided assistance to shape the narrative. Two anonymous reviewers made constructive comments. The book would be much less colorful without the wonderful photos provided by a set of photographers who are adept at their craft. Each image is a result of patient hours in the field. Parts of this book were written at Namib Rand Nature Reserve in Namibia and at the Game and Wildlife Conservation Trust in England. My son, Tristan, deserves gratitude and some meaningful father-son time for letting me disappear into the writing room for hours on end. Thanks to my wife, Kelly Powell, for telling me to rewrite the first draft in my own voice. It is possible that she was correct.

It has been my pleasure to seek the truth about birds and how they use our landscapes with a set of generous colleagues over the years: my graduate advisers William Clark, Erwin Klaas, David Krementz, and Michael Conroy; field research collaborators Mark Vrtiska and Walter Schacht; ecologists George Gale, Andrew Tyre, John Carroll, Kevin Pope, T.J. Fontaine, David

Wedin, and Mark Pegg; and seven handfuls of undergraduate researchers, graduate students, and postdocs. All have provided insights and support that have inspired information provided in this volume. Finally, my research career would not have been the same had it not been for my mentor and colleague, Mary Bomberger Brown, who has modeled a life driven by service to feathered and unfeathered friends everywhere.

Sources of the Native American legend stories:

"Prairie-chicken Dance Origin" told by Garan Coons, Sioux dancer, at Burwell, Nebraska, 2012. Recorded by Larkin Powell.

"Why the Crow Is Black" told by Good White Buffalo at Winner, Rosebud Indian Reservation, South Dakota, 1964. Recorded and transcribed by Richard Erdoes in Richard Erdoes and Alfonso Ortiz, *American Indian Myths and Legends* (New York: Pantheon, 1984).

"Why the Curlew's Bill Is Long and Crooked" is a Blackfoot legend, recorded and transcribed in Frank B. Linderman, *Indian Why Stories: Sparks from War Eagle's Lodge-Fire* (Lincoln: University of Nebraska Press, 2004).

I came face-to-face with migrating birds in the Great Plains for the first time in 1987. It was late March of my first year of college at a small school in southern Iowa and time for spring break. My friends had been planning trips to Colorado for skiing or to the Texas coast for beach lounging. I was an Iowa farm boy, and either option sounded exciting. However, upon breaking the news to my parents, I was informed that I was mistaken as to my spring break activities. Rather, I was, somewhat forcibly, invited to travel to Kearney, Nebraska, with my father to witness the migration of the sandhill cranes.

I should pause here to note that I grew up watching birds with my mother at our feeders, and my father and brother and I enjoyed going on pheasant hunts from time to time. The farm of my youth was a haven for birds, because my parents designed it with grassed terraces and waterways, ponds, and alternate strips of corn and soybeans to be soil and water friendly. However, my basic ornithological background did little to convince me of the benefits of spending a week of my life apart from my friends and, instead, in the company of four hundred thousand large, gangly birds. The clipping—with a large, color photo of these cranes from the travel section of the Sunday *Des Moines Register* that had inspired my conservation-minded parents—said nothing about beaches or mountains. I am sure you can imagine my general outlook as my father and I loaded the 1981 diesel Chevrolet Silverado farm pickup with our gear and set out on the five-hour trek to reach Kearney, Nebraska. Somewhere around my current hometown of Lincoln, a mixture of snow and sleet began to pelt our windows. Like a hostage peering from a hole scratched through a prison wall, I watched white-blanketed cornfields pass as I thought of my friends who were most likely now wearing bathing suits on Padre Island.

A few more miles down the road, the trip soured even more as the truck began to sputter. A garage somewhere along Highway 30 replaced a clogged fuel filter, while another set of my friends were pounding fresh powder on the slopes of Breckenridge. Finally, we arrived in Kearney and found a small motel for the night. The next morning, we rose in the dark and traveled a few minutes to the then-thirteen-year-old Rowe Sanctuary, an Audubon nature center along the Platte River near Gibbon, Nebraska. Our guides took us to a blind along the river, and promised us an amazing spectacle. Sure, I thought; I would rather be skiing or snorkeling.

Even today, I am stubbornly slow to suggest that the next few minutes changed the path of my life. I feel hesitant to use words like "awe-inspiring" and "life-changing," but they are descriptive of the emotions that my father and I experienced on that morning in March along the Platte.

It has been thirty years, and some parts of my memories are fuzzy. I do remember it was very dark, and I remember hearing the river and a constant chatter that our guides told us came from the cranes. Hunters and bird watchers will tell you that sunrise is actually a painfully slow process if you are in the midst of darkness waiting for the sun to illuminate a subject of interest. It seemed to take forever for the first glints of daylight to rest upon the Platte that morning, but it revealed a spectacle that most Iowa farm boys only see in books.

2. Sandhill cranes fly to roost for the night on the Platte River in central Nebraska during spring migration. Photo by Tom Koerner, USFWS.

In front of our blind, stretching for as far as I could see, were birds—big birds—standing knee-deep in the braided river (figure 2). Their gray forms outlined sand bars and truly defined the river as I could see it. So many birds clogged the channel that it was difficult to see water. The birds milled about and chattered. Some appeared to be drinking, some jumping, and some slowly walking as if they were taking an early-morning stroll to stretch their legs after the long night on the river. And then, as the sun continued to climb higher in the sky, the first birds rose from the river. Even today, I wonder what it takes to be the crane that makes the first decision to leave the flock, trusting that the rest of its peers will join it in the air. "Well-defined chaos" is a good way to describe the scene as birds begin to take flight, swirling, and deciding which way they are going to travel for foraging. The sound can be almost deafening.

Those two moments—the initial view of huddled, gray forms in the twilight and the burst of flight into the sun—are the moneymakers for the guides at the viewing blinds. Those spectacular moments are why I return to the same river today with my family and friends. And those moments are why I soon forgot about my friends on the slopes of Colorado and the beaches of Texas on that crisp March morning in 1987. Only later did I learn that this display is one of the greatest secrets of the plains. Indeed, wildlife experts from around the world flock to the Platte while many Nebraskans and Great Plains residents will tell you that they have never taken time to go see the cranes.

As you explore the Great Plains, I invite you to plan for moments like this. Discover sacred places away from the bustle of humanity. Feel the power of nature under a flock of whirling snow geese, or allow a western meadowlark to serenade you on a sunny prairie slope. The Great Plains is a wonderful place to find surprises to call your own. The birds have stories to tell, and some of those stories can be found in the pages of this book. But there are other stories that only the birds can tell to you, and the birds are out there waiting for you.

My trip to see the cranes started a three-decade process of seeing the Great Plains in a new light. As a college student in 1987, I was worried about many things that are not worth printing, and I certainly was unaware of landscape forces that were affecting birds and other wildlife of the Great Plains. As my father and I drove home, we passed many farms whose owners were considering enrolling land in a new type of set-aside, agricultural subsidy program just approved by Congress in 1986, known as the farm bill. Our trip to the Platte River occurred in the midst of the economic farm crisis of the 1980s, which may explain why my parents did not think I should go skiing: a visit to an Audubon blind was cheaper than a trip to the ski slopes. Economics rule on-farm decisions, full stop. An important component of the 1986 Farm Bill was the Conservation Reserve Program, which allowed farmers to apply for a ten-year government contract that paid an annual lease for acres not planted to crops. Instead, the lease payments would ensure that parts of the landscape would be transformed as farmers replaced cropland with native grass. Soil erosion, water quality, and wildlife habitat would receive a boost. However, I was more worried about my next calculus exam.

In the 1970s, just ten to fifteen years prior to my trip to see the cranes, states in the Great Plains were undergoing a transition toward irrigated crops. In Nebraska, over the heart of the High Plains Aquifer, 1972 marked the year in which more cropland was irrigated in the state than not irrigated. It is still hard to imagine the amount of water that is deviated from streams and rivers or pumped from wells to accomplish this feat. As my father and I returned to our dryland farm in Iowa, I was oblivious to the complexities that surrounded the Platte River that we had just visited. I remember being impressed at the scale of the center-pivot machines that are the aboveground symbol of irrigation in the plains as we drove down Highway 30 near the Platte. However, I did not understand the connection between the pivots and the water that served as the nightly protection for the cranes that we had experienced. Rivers breach the Great Plains from west to east, but I also did not realize that portions of the water flowing in these rivers were reserved for agricultural irrigation, while another portion was designated to support species of birds that were of conservation concern—such as the whooping crane, piping plover, and interior population of least tern. The Endangered Species Act was only fifteen years old when I took this trip in 1987. The peaceful river valley hid that ongoing conflict over water rights. Obligations to remove water for irrigation along the length of the Platte has slowly transformed the physical nature of the river, to the point where the river has run dry a handful of summers since I moved back to the state. At the time, I was more worried about my weekly pizza-money fund and where I would be working when the college semester ended.

My father and I had worked through a small forest edge as we walked to the blind to watch the cranes land in the river. We did not realize those trees were invaders to the space they occupied, because we had not been present to watch them spread. I was unaware of the importance of the tree removal that had been started by agencies and nature organizations along the Platte. In my defense, very few people were aware of the slow but steady encroachment by eastern red-cedar in the 1970s and 1980s on the plains. Twenty years later, biologists in Kansas would analyze aerial photos to show that the landscape my father and I journeyed through in 1987 had experienced the most significant change of any period in history with regard to the portion of the landscape covered by red-cedar. Between 1955 and 1985, red-cedar had increased by almost 6 percent per year, resulting in five times the acreage covered by red-cedar over three decades. My father and I were more worried about where we were going to find dinner as we neared the Missouri River and our home state of Iowa.

Life is full of irony, because in 2001 I moved to Nebraska as a new wildlife professor with the goal of assessing how landscapes and their habitat features affect populations of birds. One of my first research projects showed how cedar infestation can affect songbird communities, and another early project demonstrated that Conservation Reserve Program acres were critical to ring-necked pheasants and greater prairie-chickens. With the benefit of time and experience, I looked at wetlands in South Dakota and the grasslands of Kansas with new appreciation. I also saw the complexities of private landowners who farm and ranch on the plains. Just as my father and I had been selfishly concerned during our trip about things that directly affected us, it is now very clear to me that landscapes of the Great Plains are changed as the result of personal decisions made on individual farms and ranches with economics in mind.

Great Plains birds? Farm and ranch decisions affect them as well. The birds that you want to experience are in a tight dance with their human counterparts who also live in the plains. How will that dance end, you may ask? We need to talk about that, so I hope you will turn the page.

This book is about the unique avian communities of the Great Plains. For some resident birds, the fascination is their connection to the land. For other species, we find intrigue in their dependence on water bodies in the plains for migratory paths. Generations of Great Plains residents have been amused and impressed by the behaviors of birds. These are birds I have come to call "mine" in the two decades I have lived on the plains. So let me share some of their stories with you.

CHAPTER ONE

The Birds

Symbols of the Great Plains

You may consider it an unfortunate fact that many grassland birds are brown. Birders call them L B J s, for Little Brown Jobs. Open grasslands enforce unique evolutionary pressures on birds—there are fewer places to hide than, for example, in a forest. Being brown is a wonderful camouflage strategy for a bird, and Great Plains birds have explored the available hues of the brown color palette thoroughly.

Grassland birds are also lonely. Rather we should say that grassland birds have to fight the problem of potential loneliness. How can they find a mate in such a large, open landscape? Some species, like the western meadowlark, solve this problem through song. My research teams have documented hearing meadowlarks' musical invitations at a distance of almost one-third of a mile during our surveys. Males of other species, like the McCown's longspur and Sprague's pipit, use aerial displays high above the sea of grass to attract their mates. Species like lesser and greater prairie-chickens and sharp-tailed grouse are more sparsely distributed than meadowlarks, longspurs, and pipits, which makes it very problematic to find a mate. Grouse could easily go all day without seeing a familiar face. To solve that dilemma, these prairie grouse species have developed unique "lekking" mating systems, in which the males gather at the same dancing or booming ground year after year to compete with other males by strutting, fighting, and vocalizing. The females come to the lek sites to find the males, and all is solved. Breeding and comparison shopping for a mate can happen in wide open spaces, and it is amazing to see the variety of techniques that different species have developed to make reproduction happen.

Common Birds of the Great Plains

Raptors, birds of prey, are among our largest birds of the plains, and they typically soar as they search for prey. We tend to notice them. The plains are home to our national bird, the bald eagle (figure 3). The white head and tail of an adult bald eagle are ironclad identifiers. Bald eagles can be found in large numbers below dams at reservoirs in the winter throughout the Great Plains. They are more likely to nest in northern states, but over the past twenty-five years, bald-eagle nesting has increased in every state of the Great Plains. Bald eagles are long-lived, and they take up to five years to gain their solid white head and tail plumage. For the first years of their lives, juveniles, not yet sporting white tails and heads, cover vast distances looking for territories, confusing birders who believe they have seen a golden eagle (figure 3). Indeed, golden eagles and immature bald eagles both have dark plumage, but look for mottled dark and light plumage under the wings of juvenile bald eagles. Golden eagles have solid dark wings with distinct white, underwing patches and are typically found only in the western Great Plains. Both eagles can inspire awe as you watch their predatory skills in action. A colleague of mine once watched a bald eagle kill a snow goose in midair over a lake. After the goose fell in the lake, the eagle was unable to lift its prey in flight, so the eagle landed and perched on the goose as it if were a raft and used the goose's wings to row it to shore. Honestly.

The burrowing owl (figure 4) may take home your vote for the cutest bird on the plains. These owls inhabit prairie dog burrows

3. Common species of the Great Plains. *From top*: adult bald eagle, juvenile bald eagle, and golden eagle. Photos by Tom Koerner, USFWS.

or holes dug by other mammals; look for them if you are visiting a prairie dog colony (figure 5). As prairie dog numbers have declined on the plains, so have burrowing owls. In contrast, the number of red-tailed hawks (figure 4) on the plains has increased to the point that you may be able to make a game of counting them as you drive down interstate highways. Watch for them on center-pivot irrigation rigs, telephone poles, or fence posts, in addition to trees, and keep track of how many you see per mile driven. If you are a fan of European cathedrals or the animated *Hunchback of Notre Dame* movie, you will understand why my wife calls these stoic sentries the Gargoyles of the Plains. Red-tails rarely turn around to show you their unique, rusty, upper tail feathers (that would be too easy), so look for the streaked, dark chest stripe on their lower chest that distinguishes them from other perching raptors. Another movie note: if you enjoy westerns that feature soaring bald eagles with shrill screams that echo through the valleys, Hollywood is attempting to trick you as the director has dubbed a red-tailed hawk's call into the film. The mighty bald eagle's true vocalization is less worthy of the cinema than its proud silhouette.

Rough-legged hawks (figure 4) are arctic breeders that can be seen in large numbers on the plains only during spring and fall migration or during the winter. Dark patches on the underside of their wings can assist with identifications. Their name is derived from feathers that extend down their legs. Ferruginous hawks (figure 4), named for the rusty (ferrous) color on their wings, breed only on the plains and mountain states to the immediate west, and they also have feathers that extend down their legs. A sighting of a fuzzy-legged hawk in the summer is most likely this species. As you pass through wide, open prairie on your travels, keep your eyes peeled for a ferruginous's large stick nest in a lone tree or on a windmill or power pole.

4. Common species of the Great Plains. *From top*: burrowing owl (Bart van Dorp, CCL), red-tailed hawk, *left* (Rodney Campbell, CCL), rough-legged hawk, *right* (Tom Koerner, USFWS), and ferruginous hawk (Troy Williams, CCL).

5. A burrowing owl and its chick rest outside the burrow of a prairie dog on a prairie in New Mexico. Photo by Dick Thompson.

The upland sandpiper (figure 6) is, as its name implies, a shorebird, but it is not found near water. Instead, you will most likely see these birds standing atop a fencepost. If you wander too close to their ground nests on a prairie walk, the pair will let you know by circling and calling above your head. Their chicks are *precocial*, which means each chick is feathered and ready to walk as soon as they hatch from their egg. The hatchlings follow the parents as they learn to forage for insects. Researchers in Kansas have found that upland sandpipers, like other precocial species such as ducks, pheasants, and grouse, commonly take their newly hatched chicks up to a quarter of a mile from the nest to find food on the first day of the chicks' lives outside of the eggshell. Imagine heading out on that journey in the first few hours under the sun.

Horned larks (figure 6) are an example of a plains-dwelling bird that prefers less-dense stands of grass for foraging, and you may see them in areas with bare ground caused by grazing or

6. Common species of the Great Plains. *From top, left to right*: upland sandpiper (Larkin Powell), horned lark (Joel Jorgensen), bobolink (Joel Jorgensen), yellow-headed blackbird (Ryan Moehring, usfws), grasshopper sparrow (Andrew Weitzel, ccl), and loggerhead shrike (D. Alexander).

haying, agricultural tillage, or another disturbance. You may not see the male's hornlike feathers through your binoculars. In contrast to the upland sandpiper, a horned lark has *altricial* young, which means each nestling hatches from its egg in a naked, eyes-closed, and defenseless state. After eight to ten days in the nest, however, the young are soon bailing from the nest to follow the parents with short hops and flutters.

Bobolinks (figure 6) breed in the northern plains, and you will most likely find them in meadows or other areas of dense, open grasslands. If you find one, look for others as they crowd into good nesting areas. Like all grassland birds, bobolinks need grasslands with an array of flowering plants—it is not enough to have a monoculture of grassland, as you might find in a seeded pasture, for example. Birds do not depend on the flowers for aesthetic reasons, although it may be interesting to ponder what birds find "beautiful." Instead, the flowers attract a host of insects that are the primary protein source to feed nestlings and growing fledglings. More flowers in a pasture means more ants and aphids and beetles, and that means happy, healthy baby birds with full tummies. If you can visualize how fast a human baby grows, consider that a nestling bobolink grows from about 3 grams to 22 grams in less than fourteen days. The juveniles are eating, pooping, and growing machines, doubling in size every three to four days. (Human babies take three months to double in size for the first time, thankfully!) A bobolink fledgling's legs are about three-quarters of adult length when they leave the nest, which allows them to hop about and follow their parents. However, their wings and tail are less than half of their eventual adult length. The wings and tail will continue to grow rapidly with the high-protein diet of insects from their parents.

Your first sighting of a male yellow-headed blackbird (figure 6), accented in a marsh by the morning sun, can be magical. They tend to be found in wetlands with more open water than their cousin, the red-winged blackbird, prefers. Females are drabber than males with only a bit of yellow on their head, and the pattern of drab females is common among birds and especially grassland birds. Why? Imagine trying to hide your nest from a potential predator with a bright yellow set of feathers on your head. Over thousands of generations, females with brighter feathers have been removed from the gene pool by a variety of predators, while males with showy plumage are rewarded with more offspring who carry on their father's trait. The females do not need to show off, as they are the ones making the choice for a mate in most cases. Males compete with other males for the attention of females using their plumage as a guide to their prowess as a potential mate. Parasites that live in feathers can plague birds, which is a really good reason to wash your hands if you ever handle a live bird, and these parasites tend to destroy the integrity of their hosts' feathers making them duller in color. Therefore, males with bright feathers may also be signaling to females that their genes allow them to be less prone to parasitic infections. Along with straight teeth and a college education, avoidance of parasitic infections is something every mother bird wants for her offspring.

Grasshopper sparrows (figure 6) get their name because their song includes a trill that sounds very much like their namesake insect. Odds are, you may hear them before you see them darting from one grass clump to another. Drab in color, the grasshopper sparrow may be the Little Brown Job poster bird. The song of this smallish sparrow will either become one of your favorites or start to drive you crazy, as grasshopper sparrows are one of the most abundant sparrows in the Great Plains. Early pioneers learned to love this bird because the sparrows ate loads of grasshoppers that plagued the farmers' fields.

If you are looking for the dark, evil overlord of the plains, then you have found your spirit animal in the loggerhead shrike (figure 6). Shrikes, found throughout the Great Plains, are the

7. A prairie lizard (male) impaled on a barbed-wire fence in the Great Plains is a good indicator that a shrike is nearby. Photo by Larkin Powell.

8. Common species of the Great Plains. *From top*: wild turkey (USDA), northern bobwhite (Andrew Morffew, CCL), and scissor-tailed flycatcher (Randy Hesford).

size of a robin with the heart of a red-tailed hawk. These sneaky predators eat small rodents, lizards, other birds, and insects. Keep an eye on barbed-wire fences or thorn bushes as you hike—shrikes are famous for impaling their prey as a way of storing the food for a later snack. If you see a lizard, small snake, or grasshopper hanging lifeless from a barb on a fence, you might look around for nearby shrikes (figure 7).

The wild turkey is now found in all of the forty-eight continental states of the U.S. and Hawaii (figure 8). Starting in the 1950s and 1960s, state wildlife agencies in the Southeast traded some of their turkeys to northern states for Canada geese or river otters. All of these transplants have been very successful. Our airports are now overrun with Canada geese, and kayakers can find river otters back in their former range. Benjamin Franklin positioned the wild turkey as an intelligent bird worthy for consideration as our national bird, and each fall and spring, turkeys outsmart over half of the hunters who take to the fields in search of Sunday dinner. Throughout the Great Plains in the winter, you can find mixed flocks of ten to fifty (or more) males, females, and immature turkeys. In spring, watch for males strutting near woodlands at the edge of pastures or crop fields as they try to attract females for mating.

The northern bobwhite (figure 8) may not provide such a visually impressive display as does their cousin, the turkey, but these small quail rely on vocalizations to find mates. The countryside in spring and summer can be pierced by their two-note, namesake call, "bob-white!" Try carrying on a conversation with them if you hear one calling—whether the male sees you as a threat or even recognizes your whistle is questionable, but it can be fun to try. Bobwhite are found in respectable numbers from Nebraska south across the Great Plains, and they are susceptible to habitat loss and harsh winters. You may appreciate their presence more when you learn that in an average year,

9. A scissor-tailed flycatcher uses its tail feathers to make quick turns in flight, shown here capturing an insect. Photo by Diane Brown.

over 90 percent of bobwhites may find their way into a coyote's stomach or some other cause of death. Nature is red in tooth and claw, as the poet Tennyson wrote. Typically, only a quarter of nests of most species of bird are successful in producing offspring, so female bobwhites who lose their first nest will lay another clutch of eggs as they try to produce enough young to keep up with their mortality level. It is a tough world out there on the plains.

Scissor-tailed flycatchers are a proud breeding bird of the southern plains (figure 8), but they are rebellious at heart, wandering east, west, and north (as far north as Nova Scotia) on their migration between Central America and the southern plains. Their unique tail and body form make the species easy to spot (figure 9) on fences or electric lines as you zip along the highway during spring and summer. If you find one, and slow down for a good look, you may quickly add them to your list of favorite birds because of their pinkish flanks, smooth gray head, and long black-and-white tail.

Mating and Breeding Behaviors

Bird watching can be viewed as a multilevel sport. The entry level involves noticing birds from time to time, especially strange or unusual birds that we encounter. The second level is defined by a bird watcher who runs about and finds as many species as possible: list-making. However, once a bird has been found, there is an opportunity to learn more about the bird—an opportunity to let the bird talk to you and tell you about its life. Thus, the third level of bird watching involves prolonged observation.

What little quirks does the bird have? Maybe it twerks its tail every few seconds—why does it do that? Maybe it crawls head-down along a tree trunk—what is it doing? Perhaps it flits out away from a tree and flits quickly back—what is the purpose of these little flights? This is the realm of bird behavior.

As we discuss behaviors of birds, I am going to break a golden rule held by many ornithologists: *thou shalt not ascribe human qualities and thoughts to birds*. Strictly, it is true that without experimentation it is impossible to know the real function for the behaviors we see in birds. However, I want to encourage you to think about why birds do what they do. Make a guess. The father of wildlife management, Aldo Leopold, enjoyed watching wildlife on walks near his cabin in Wisconsin, and he wrote descriptive passages in which he used humanlike actions to describe the animals around him. Regarding the death of a rabbit on a warm January day, Leopold wrote in *A Sand County Almanac*: "To this rabbit the thaw brought freedom from want, but also a reckless abandonment of fear. The owl has reminded him that thoughts of spring are no substitute for caution."

As we watch animal behavior, we do need to keep in mind that our conclusions about the events unfolding before us may be quite false. It is hard to get inside the brain of a bird. Consider an alien life-form landing its invisible spacecraft in the grassy space of a very large city park in which a group of yoga enthusiasts have gathered for their Yoga-in-the-Park exercise session. The yoga session begins, and the class follows the leader in a series of poses, extending their arms toward the rising sun, raising their arms to the sky, and then squatting. Clearly, the alien surmises, the group is training for combat, and their commander is forcing them through odd rituals to suppress all individualistic tendencies. Of course, they are simply exercising. Our understanding of bird behavior may be as poor as an alien's understanding of yoga, but if we try to think like a bird and imagine a list of possible explanations for what we observe, we cannot help but close the gap that often exists between humans and the world around us.

To pique your interest in bird behavior, in the next section I have chosen five species to describe that are common targets of bird watchers and tourists on the Great Plains. Focus your attention on their behaviors shown in the sketches by Allison Johnson, a research ornithologist; her insights from hours in the field with birds guide her artwork.

Sandhill Crane Stick Throwing

Sandhill cranes mate for multiple breeding seasons, which some people interpret with the phrase "mate for life." If you could avoid adopting that terminology, it would be best. Many interpret the mating behaviors of species such as swans and cranes to mean that when a mate dies, the other individual dons a black outfit and mourns for the rest of their days, like the English Queen Victoria when her beloved Albert passed away. In fact, swans and cranes do form a pair bond that lasts longer than a single breeding season. However, there are always exceptions to the rule. Birds go astray with infidelities, and if a mate dies,

10. Sandhill crane stick-throwing behavior. Drawing by Allison Johnson.

the other individual usually finds a new mate. Reproducing is the major goal of life, you see. All mating behaviors—including mate attraction, copulation with a nonmate, pair bonds, and parental behavior— are for one purpose: reproducing as much as possible.

You will most likely encounter cranes in the Great Plains on their way north. At any given time during spring migration, there are some young cranes finding their first mate and older cranes seeking to confirm their pair bond. Because of this, spring migration is filled with a lot of fun-to-watch dancing and shaking among the cranes. Crane dancing may involve bowing, wing stretching, and jumping or running. If you find a flock of cranes in a field or wetland during migration, spend some time looking for these behaviors. At first, the flock may look like they are all feeding, but soon you will see the hanky-panky happening. And it is important hanky-panky.

Cranes and other birds use mating displays to reduce physical fighting. As you heard from your third-grade teacher when you punched the bully who pushed you down the hill and covered your face with mud, fighting doesn't solve any problems—you just end up bruised and you still hate the other person. Fighting between animals is risky: they could win or they could be injured or die. Much better to hop around and make funny faces and point to the treetops and then your shoelaces to show your prowess. Male birds hope that a fancy and fitful display will tell the other males that a fight is not worth the effort—they would be beaten. In this manner, many fights are averted, but not all. There is still sometimes a need for third-grade teachers to pull them apart.

You will also see male and female birds performing courtship rituals in addition to the actual act of mating. As an example, mated pairs of sandhill cranes often do "unison calling"— throwing back their heads at the same time and cackling to the clouds above. It is simply their manner, we ornithologists believe, of telling each other that they are still there and still interested in the other. "I love you so much that I will do this ridiculous display," they are saying, we think. By this behavior, their bond is further strengthened.

And then there is stick throwing—another way to confirm the pair bond. Either the male or female will pinch a stick, a corncob, a corn stalk, or other sticklike object with their bill and toss it into the air (figure 10). Some biologists believe that the birds are so excited about nest building that they simulate picking up sticks to build a nest as they migrate toward their nesting grounds. Whatever the reason, stick throwing is one of my favorite bird behaviors to watch.

The Dance of the Western Grebe

We all have an amazing person in our life who we think can walk on water, and western grebes insist on this trait in their mates. In contrast to the longer pair bonds of cranes, grebes find new mates each year. Thus, the journey north to the breeding grounds is a time to display, impress the opposite sex, and form pairs. During migration, you can observe grebes and their mating behaviors on larger, deeper lakes.

The mating dance of the western grebe is called "rushing." Individuals begin by facing each other with bellies on the water. Then they point their bills at each other, with heads up or straight out along the water, while making loud, staccato "tic" vocalizations. Suddenly, one individual will twist sideways, hold their wings stiffly to the back, rise up, and scamper across the surface of the water (figure 11). The second individual will quickly follow and catch up. The synchronized scampering that ensues is a display that is almost unbelievable. The rushers may be two males, a male and a female, or more than one male and a female. The dance is over in about four to five seconds and

11. Mating dance of the western grebe. Drawing by Allison Johnson.

only lasts for about fifty to sixty feet. I have tried to do this, and it is quite difficult. In fact, I do not even have a personal record for distance yet, but it is fun to try and good exercise.

We know that grebes' feet hit the water up to twenty times per second during these rushes, because biologists have used high-speed filming of the dance to get a better view. The slap of the webbed foot on the surface, along with a quick push with each foot into the water, keeps the birds on the surface of the lake. As with other displays in the world of birds, it is likely that the display serves to provide potential mates with an idea of which male is best built and thus a more acceptable mate. Coordinated dancing between males and females may serve to strengthen the forming pair bond.

Greater and Lesser Prairie-Chicken Dance

The competition between males that occurs at prairie-chicken lek sites can be furious. The prime location is the middle of the lek, and the males here typically end up participating in at least 80 percent of the copulations at the lek. Those males pass on their genes to the next generation, and research from Kansas reveals that the males who obtain the more central locations are really the prime individuals from the standpoint of genetic quality. Just as cattle breeders use the best bull to fertilize their cows, prairie-chickens have a system that almost guarantees that females who pay attention to location will get the best product available that year. As my wife likes to joke, "If you do not have real estate, you do not mate." I am pretty sure she is talking about prairie-chickens.

Lek-based mating systems are used by some species of antelope, bats, frogs, and moths, and the behaviors at leks of any species are always quite dramatic. All of the males have gathered in one spot, it is breeding season, and everything is on the line. Think of a dance club for college students and remember back

12. Mating dance of the greater prairie-chicken. Drawing by Allison Johnson.

to the crazy dancing you did at that age. I apologize for bringing that up, but now you understand the dynamic. Females get the information they need, and we enjoy it when we have the opportunity to peek into their world for a moment. I may be biased because I have studied prairie-chickens in Nebraska for over a decade, but I feel that the mating displays of grouse on the Great Plains are some of the most visually appealing behaviors to watch.

Lesser prairie-chickens are a bit smaller than greater prairie-chickens and lessers are found in the southern plains, while greaters are found in the north. However, their dances are similar, and males start to gather at lek sites each morning in mid-January. In February, they really get serious about demarcating the lek site into display territories, and in March the females start to arrive at the lek. Females will land near the lek, which sends all of the males into a complete frenzy. If you are watching a lek site in the spring, a sudden increase in volume and activity in the males is a sure sign that a female has landed nearby. The female prairie-chicken has lessons to share regarding self-confidence and dignity in the face of peer pressure. Gracefully, she will walk through the lek, looking over the males, turning her back on them, one by one. Most days, all will be shunned, and the males will go back to squabbling over borders again. Eventually, the day comes for the female to make a decision, and she chooses. More often than not, a nearby male may come in to try to force his opinion onto the situation, which may throw all plans askew for a moment. Eventually, a copulation occurs.

Males have a variety of behaviors at the lek. When females are present, males will make short jumps into the air, called flutter jumping, associated with shorter high-pitched whoop vocalizations. They rarely flutter-jump without a female on the lek. "Over here, over here," they seem to be saying with their leaps. "You should walk over here to check me out."

The main booming display involves foot stomping (watch their feet and listen for the repetitive thump sounds), raised feathers on the neck (called pinnae feathers because they appear like large ears) that expose orange air sacs, stiffened tail feathers (figure 12), and booming vocalizations that use the air sacs to produce a low frequency sound. From a distance, the booms sound like someone blowing on a pop bottle. Through your binoculars, the male prairie-chickens will appear like a wide U with their pinnae feathers and their tail raised vertically. In landscapes where prairie-chickens overlap with sharp-tailed grouse, you can distinguish the sharp-tailed grouse as an L shape from their vertical tail and outstretched head that is lacking the long pinnae feathers of the prairie-chicken.

The boom sound echoes over the landscape, and on a still morning, it is possible to hear a prairie-chicken lek at a distance of one mile or a bit more. On the lek, the birds are alternating between scuffling, stare-downs with neighbors, or just standing or sitting while they wait for the next action to start. Small leks of two or three birds occur in some places, and there are reports of single males dancing by themselves; the largest lek in our study site in southeast Nebraska had almost seventy males. That was a busy place.

Sharp-Tailed Grouse Mating Dance

In South Dakota, western Nebraska, North Dakota, and northeastern Colorado, sharp-tailed grouse share the prairie with greater prairie-chickens. However, the range of sharp-tailed grouse continues across Montana and most of Canada. Similar to their cousins, sharp-tailed grouse males also gather for mating dances in the spring, but their dance is unique. Sharp-tailed grouse have a namesake, pointed tail (figure 13; prairie-chickens have an evenly rounded tail), and the two longest feathers actually are whacked against each other at high rates of speed to

13. Mating dance of the sharp-tailed grouse. Drawing by Allison Johnson.

create a buzzing sound when the males dance. Try making this motion with two of your fingers. It is difficult to imagine the muscles in their tail that make their feathers snap together so quickly. Sharpies, as we can call them after we gain their trust, have purple air sacs, compared to the orange air sacs of prairie-chickens. If you are farther away, the most obvious difference is that sharpies dance with their wings outstretched. When they have their wings out, tail up, head pointed straight forward, and their feet pounding the ground, one of my friends tells me she thinks they look just like a windup toy careening around the prairie. See if you think she is right the next time you are at a sharp-tailed grouse lek.

Plover Broken-Wing Display

Four species of plovers breed and nest on the plains: the ubiquitous killdeer, piping plover in the northern plains, mountain plover in the western plains, and snowy plover in the southern plains. These plovers all share a nesting behavior that is designed to protect their nest from predators. Imagine the issues with placing a nest on the ground—it is not hidden in a cavity of a tree or in a hole in the ground and it is not elevated to relative safety in the branches of a bush or tree. Any snake, mammal, or avian predator has easy access to the ground nest. To combat the predators, these small birds have developed a distraction behavior: they feign a broken wing, as they seem to drag themselves along the ground (figure 14). Often the broken-wing display is accompanied by loud calling as another form of distraction, which may be enough to make the predator forget about the potential for a tasty pile of eggs nearby, and the plover will eventually fly off after taking the predator a safe distance from the nest. Some individuals have another trick—they do what is called false brooding. If the plover sees a coyote approaching, the plover will slip silently off the nest and scurry to a nearby

14. Piping plover broken-wing display. Drawing by Allison Johnson.

location and pretend to sit on a nonexistent nest. The predator is more likely to see the bird than its eggs, and the plover can then fly away revealing an empty patch of earth to the frustration of the coyote or other predator.

The broken-wing display of a plover is only effective if the nesting bird can see the predators and has time to react. Therefore, plovers not only nest on the ground but select nesting sites that are fairly flat and have little vegetation within a radius of about thirty feet, which is apparently the distance they need to recognize predators and take action. Their eggs are highly camouflaged in color, blending in with the surrounding gravel or sand.

What triggers the broken-wing display? Many bird behaviors are innate, or reflex responses, which is similar to the way human babies who will suck when anything is placed in their mouth. The automatic sucking behavior assures that our babies will eat. Biologists refer to these behaviors as hardwired, in contrast to behaviors that require thought and decisions. The section of birds' brains that is responsible for reflex behaviors is large, compared to mammals. Female geese have a reflex behavior to roll eggs back into the nest with their bill, but they can be triggered to perform the same behavior by placing a rock or a golf ball near the nest. Scientists have also quickly removed eggs from the vicinity of a nest, and the mother goose will make egg-rolling motions in the absence of an egg. Such behaviors do not suggest that geese, or birds in general, are stupid. Far from it—crows and jays have the ability to solve complex problems that require thought and planning. But these reflex behaviors provide a wonderful insight into the complexities of animal brains.

Is the broken-wing display of a plover a reflex or is it a result of active decision-making? Does the nesting bird automatically run from the nest and droop its wing at the sight of a predator? As we might predict, a biologist did an experiment and found that plovers will change their strategy for nest protection in accordance with the type of predator that is approaching. For example, cattle are not a threat to nest contents unless the cow steps on the nest, so plovers will not perform a broken-wing display if a cow approaches the nest. Instead, the nesting bird will hunker down to determine if the nest is in danger of an offending hoof, and the bird will fly up in a flutter to surprise the bovine interloper and cause it to stumble in a different direction. More evidence for the behavior being a conscious decision is that the broken-wing display is usually made while the bird looks over its back at the predator. If the predator is not falling for the ruse, the plover will often engage the predator by approaching it in an attempt to create a better distraction. Therefore, the broken-wing display is a tool that plovers use from a complex toolbox of behaviors and adaptations developed to protect their nests.

CHAPTER TWO

The Place

Homes, Habitats, and Aerial Highways

A few years ago, my brother-in-law invited us to Montana to celebrate his wedding in August. We took the opportunity to support our nation's railway system, such as it is. We booked seats on Amtrak leaving Minneapolis, Minnesota, to cross the prairies and navigate the mountains past Glacier National Park on our way to the town of Libby, Montana. We boarded in the dark of night, as is the tradition with Amtrak, and we found our seats and slept as best we could. The train lumbered northwest to Fargo and Grand Forks, North Dakota, and as day broke, we turned west and headed past Devils Lake. I found a coffee and pastry for breakfast, and I selected a seat in the observation car—the one with the domed windows that allow Amtrak passengers to view America as it slides by. I was thrilled to realize that I was in the midst of the Prairie Pothole wetland system. In the morning light, all manner of ducks were splashing about, feeding, and having a wonderful time being ducks. I quickly spotted mallards, blue-winged teal, northern pintails, and northern shovelers. For a wildlife biologist, it was a morning that could not have been planned and timed better. But those seated around me did not seem to agree with my sentiments.

"This is completely flat," said one teenager. "There's nothing out there."

"Yes, I know," his father answered. "We'll be in the mountains soon enough, so just read your book and watch the sunrise."

The Great Plains is often described as "flyover country," because some folks do not like to drive through the region. Apparently, for some, the train ride is also a burden. Of course, there were plenty of somethings out there, beyond our train's windows, but the landscape was admittedly short on trees, tall buildings, and mountains.

That empty landscape is home to a host of birds, which make use of grasslands, wetlands, linear forests, and river corridors— the main habitats for breeding birds in the Great Plains. A glance at a map of North American land cover (figure 15) shows that the Great Plains is, today, primarily cropland and grazed rangelands. And the plains region is obviously represented by different colors on the map than areas to the west or east. How is it that the plains are so different from the rest of North America? To answer that, we need to take a quick journey in time.

Deep History: Feathers, Then Birds, Then Great Plains

Birds are ancient creatures, but they are relatively new in terms of geologic time on earth. If you can imagine the entire 4.5-billion-year history of the earth as a twenty-four-hour clock, the Great Plains starts its unique existence in a submerged state, beneath an inland sea at about thirty minutes until midnight (approximately 85 million years ago). Prior to this, the area-to-be-subsequently-known-as-the-Great-Plains had wandered about the face of the earth as continents drifted apart, rammed together, and gave each other odd group names like Pangea, Laurasia, and Gondwana.

The soon-to-be-plains rested on an ocean floor, and the sea split the western and eastern regions of modern-day North America (figure 15). On the other side of the globe, in the area of present-day China, dinosaurs with primitive featherlike

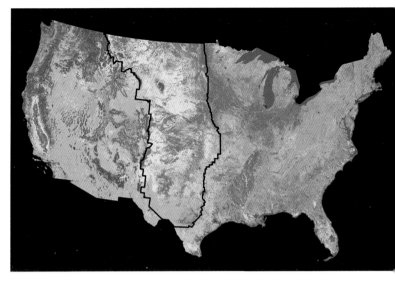

15. Land cover of the United States, overlaid by the boundaries of the Great Plains region. Within the plains, the darkest shade of *green* is the pine forests of the Black Hills in South Dakota. Crop fields are darker brown than the light-colored rangelands. Land-cover data from USGS.

structures were starting to make fashion statements. With fifteen minutes left in the twenty-four-hour day of the earth's existence, the Rocky Mountains had risen to our west and the first signs of true birds appeared in aquatic habitats on the edge of the draining, drying, inland sea. Dinosaurs with birdlike features roamed the exposed land areas as the Great Plains continued to dry, and true flying birds appeared in the core of the Great Plains at five minutes until midnight. With ninety seconds left in the twenty-four-hour earth day, modern sister species of birds that bookend the Great Plains, such as indigo and lazuli buntings or eastern and western meadowlarks, had differentiated as separate species.

Although the twenty-four-hour clock gives us a relative sense of time, it may be a misleading metaphor as all of these activities were, of course, happening about as fast as I peddle a bicycle uphill. Each hour of the twenty-four-hour clock scenario is worth about 180 million years and each minute represents 3 million years. So, relative to the history of the earth, birds are a flash in the pan, but they have a long history measured in real years. The two meadowlark species in the plains split over 2 million years ago, for example. It is really quite difficult to comprehend how long eastern and western meadowlarks, as we now refer to them, have been brightening mornings and evenings on the plains. If your kids complain that it is taking "for-ev-er" to cross Kansas, just tell them that in geologic time, you are traveling at Mach speed.

Indeed, everything is relative, as Einstein suggested. The fossil record of the first *Homo sapiens* on the other side of the globe dates to only 250,000 years ago (in the last five seconds of the earth's twenty-four-hour clock!), and humans first walked onto the Great Plains about 15,000 years ago. The birds were here first.

I have a colleague who studies reptiles, and he likes to remind me that birds are just "reptiles that have gone bad." In a way, he is correct. Birds are thought to have developed from a group of dinosaurs that developed feathers, and we can look at the scales on birds' legs today and see a similarity to reptiles. In fact, feathers are simply scales that were modified over millions of years. There were feathers before there were birds, which might also suggest that the egg did indeed precede the chicken. Based on layers of ash in which feathered dinosaurs were found in China, we know that feathers have been adorning reptilelike animals for at least 120 million years. The first feathers were not for flight, but are thought to have provided insulation to their bearers. Early feathers were colored, which suggests that these feathered dinosaurs may also have used feathers for displaying, a function that plumage still has today.

The oceans slipped away from our region, because the Rocky Mountains were building in the west during a period of volcanic activity and uprising of the edges of tectonic plates. As soon as new rock formations appeared, they started to erode, and sands and other sediments flowed east from the Rockies. Gradually, the sloping base of the plains was formed so that by 50 million years ago, the foundations of the basic landscape that we know as the plains had been set. During the geologically busy period of 135 to 65 million years ago, the fossil record provides evidence of the transition from dinosaurs to birds in the Great Plains. Pterosaurs, the first nonfeathered reptiles known to achieve powered flight with wings of skin stretched between their ankles and elongated arms, can be found in museums in the southern Great Plains. The massive *Dakotaraptor* wandered the landscapes of present-day South Dakota (figure 16). Its tail-to-snout length of eighteen feet was the same as a modern-day sport utility vehicle or bass boat. The large feathers on their legs contrasted with the featherless legs of other dinosaurs such as *Tyrannosaurus* and *Triceratops* that lived in the same time and place.

Before dinosaurs disappeared 66 million years ago, true birds started to emerge on the drying lands that would eventually become the Great Plains. An ancestor to modern flamingos waded in Wyoming. Deposits in Kansas have revealed fossils of a flightless bird that may have looked similar to a diving cormorant of today and a flying ternlike bird, *Ichthyornis*. The latter bird is a unique fossil record, as *Ichthyornis* retained teeth left over from its dinosaur ancestors, but it also had the skull design of a modern-day bird with muscle attachment points on its skull and bone structures that allowed it to use its beaklike pinchers. Lurching forward in time, cousins to the modern day sandhill cranes have been found in fossil beds in western Nebraska that date to 10 million years ago, and in that general

16. A life restoration of the eighteen-foot long *Dakotaraptor* by Emily Willoughby.

time period the fossil records for birds explodes: a loon, a cormorant, a flamingo, ducks, swan-sized waterfowl, a vulture, a condor, an owl, hawks, kites, quail, grouse, and sandpipers. These are species that are similar but not the same as modern-day birds—their ancestors presumably.

The period between 100 million and 10 million years, therefore, would have been an amazing time for a time-traveling ornithologist to watch changes taking place in dinosaurs and the development of birds on the emerging plains. We can safely state that 10 to 15 million years ago, flocks of recognizable bird species were flapping their wings on the landscapes of the Great Plains. A fossil deposit in south-central Nebraska, dated to approximately 2 million years ago, revealed a list of familiar species of birds that a modern bird watcher would love to spot on an outing: a pied-billed grebe, green-winged teal, northern harrier, ferruginous hawk, wild turkey, long-eared owl, and the now extinct passenger pigeon. Also included in the large fossil deposit was a ptarmigan, now found in Alaska. This cousin to the prairie-chicken bred in the grasslands and spruce forests of the region just to the west of the towering glaciers during the Ice Age, in the midst of mammoths, mastodons, and musk oxen.

Establishing the Unique Landscapes of the Great Plains

What was physically happening to the Great Plains as birds arrived on the scene? Why is the Great Plains relatively flat? What caused wetlands and rivers to form? Why do many rivers in the plains run to the east?

We can go back to the period in which the inland sea covered the region. To simplify the geology, I want you to think about the Great Plains as an empty sandbox—the kind you had as a kid in the backyard. Imagine you have used your mom's garden hose to fill it with water. That is the inland sea, and if you want to add details, like large sharks swimming in the swamped sandbox, you can. Now we go away and let the sun dry out the watery mess we have made in the sandbox. Perhaps your father decides to get a load of sand to add to the sandbox. Like all busy fathers, he dumps it into the sandbox from one side, starts to spread it out a bit, but is distracted by another chore in the yard. So we have a sandbox with more sand on one side than the other. It is a big slope.

That is exactly (a geologist would argue with "exactly") how the eroded deposits from the Rocky Mountains filled the area of the former inland sea. In almost every way possible, these deposits of sediment define the plains and affect the birds and other animals that are found in the region. And they affect you, as you drive about.

Our sandbox has a large slope from one side to the other—the Great Plains slopes downhill from the Rockies eastward. Over time, as you spray more water over your newly filled sandbox, rivers and streams are cut into the sediments. The Great Plains is marked by many west-to-east rivers (the Platte, the Kansas, the Arkansas, the Cimarron, the Canadian, the Red) that head downhill quickly. As an example, the Platte River descends at about seven feet per mile, which you will not notice as you drive down Interstate 80. By comparison, the mighty Mississippi River only drops a little over two inches per mile as it heads from Minnesota to the Gulf Coast. The elevation of Plattsmouth, Nebraska, where the Platte empties into the Missouri River, is 981 feet above sea level, according to Google. North Platte in western Nebraska and the confluence of the North and South Platte Rivers, has an elevation of 2,802 feet, and Google will also tell you that the two cities are 276 miles apart: hence the drop of seven feet per mile. Denver, 290 miles west of North Platte, has an exact elevation of one mile, or 5,280 feet. The drop from Denver to North Platte is 8.5 feet per mile, so the slope is steeper closer to the mountains. Interstates 94, 90, 80, 70, and 40 are built on the sloping slag pile of rubble that has come east from the Rockies over millions of years. The sandy debris continues to be moved downstream by water today, creating sandbars and unique riverine habitats for shorebirds and waterfowl. Those west-to-east rivers, driven by the gradual sloping of the plains, serve as stopover points in ladderlike fashion as birds migrate north and south. It turns out that geology has a big impact on geese, ducks, shorebirds, and cranes.

Now that you have sprinkled more water on the sand in your sandbox, consider what happened to that water. Some of it ran off, creating the little rivers we noted above, but some of the water sank into the sand, where it was trapped between the tiny particles. Even if you come back to your sandbox in a week, you will most likely find moist sand if you burrow beneath the surface. In similar fashion, the loose sediments from the Rockies consolidated to create water-bearing geologic formations that form the basement to the Great Plains. Recent controversies about oil pipelines have raised familiarity with another defining feature of the Great Plains, the High Plains Aquifer, often referred to as the Ogallala Aquifer (figure 17). The aquifer functions just like the water held by the moist sand in your sandbox.

In some regions, such as the Nebraska Sandhills, the aquifer peeks above the surface of the ground to create large lakes and wetlands. The economic future of many farmers in the Great Plains is tied to the presence and sustainability of the aquifer. Those farmers make decisions about how much water is drawn from the aquifer each year for irrigation, and the groundwater-fed streams, wetlands, and ponds provide unique habitat for breeding and migratory birds in the central and southern plains. Aquifer levels in the southern plains have dropped precipitously in recent years, which will affect land use and bird life in the near future. In the central plains, many streams stay ice-free during the winter

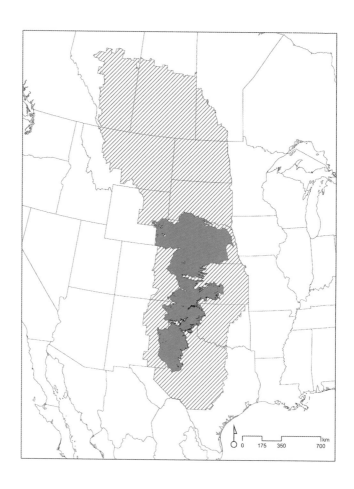

17. The position of the High Plains Aquifer (*dark shading*) within the
Great Plains (*hashed shading*). Public spatial data from U S G S.

because of the ground-warmed water that emerges from springs, supporting wintering trumpeter swans and other waterbirds.

"Time changes things," the Supremes sang, and the Great Plains is no exception. Glaciation is one force that has gnawed at the landscapes of the northern and eastern plains, reshaping them in their path. The glaciers smoothed landscapes as they inched south, and the brute force of the glacier completely rerouted the Missouri River, which used to run north into Canada. The current route of the Missouri marks the general edge of one glacial advance. Melting water from the massive ice sheet surged southeast along the forward face of the glacier, forming the south- and east-flowing, muddy Missouri. Glaciers also left telltale signs behind as they retreated—uneven deposits of glacial debris. The depressions, known as prairie potholes, formed by this process sit on flat land and are not fed by streams or ground water. The potholes of North and South Dakota and prairie Canada are unique to the Great Plains. The region, with its widespread wetlands surrounded by grasslands, is literally the duck factory for North America—the breeding ground for up to 70 percent of the continent's ducks.

It was this wetland landscape that I was crossing on the Amtrak when the naïve teenager declared it boring and full of nothingness. Can you imagine? Nothing could be farther from the truth if you consider the violent uprising of the Rockies to the west with the power of the glacier that plowed through and created the ponds full of duck families preparing to head south for the winter. But the ability to see the big picture is limited in all teenagers. Thankfully, they soon grow up.

Later disturbances to the sandbox of our Great Plains created other features. In the southern high plains, new sediments and wind erosion during the Pleistocene formed the shallow playa wetlands that dominate the landscape in west Texas as well as parts of New Mexico, Oklahoma, Kansas, and Colorado. The sand dunes of the Sandhills region in Nebraska are a more recent phenomenon, a result of wind-borne sediments that arrived in Nebraska after the last Ice Age. The dry uplands of the dunes support a thriving beef-cattle industry while also providing a refuge to grassland birds that have been largely extirpated from grasslands to the east that are now corn and soybean fields.

So what happened to our sandbox? All of the disturbances to the surface of the Great Plains resulted in unique rivers and a series of pondlike wetlands that span the plains. Each wetland system on the plains has a different geologic history but a similar modern-day function as nesting, migratory, and wintering habitat for birds. Many of the national wildlife refuges, state wildlife management areas, and other public spaces in the Great Plains have been developed in wetland systems.

What about the grasslands? The upraised Rocky Mountains were responsible for the prairies of the plains. Worldwide, 5 to 10 million years ago, a drying climate reduced woodland extent, and grasslands started to dominate the plains. The western plains area is in a rain shadow of the Rockies, which further dried the region. Grasses thrived and developed in shortgrass communities in the western plains and in tallgrass communities in the east, where more rain falls. Over 90 percent of larger mammals found in fossil deposits from this time have teeth that tell us they were grazing animals, and birds mingled with a large-sized mammalian community that might have reminded you of the scene from a modern-day safari in southern Africa: many species of horses, miniature pronghorns, tapirs, and rhinos. The vegetation of the plains has evolved to be grazed regularly. Bison survived the abrupt extinction of megafauna approximately 10,000 years ago and became the main grazers on the plains until the 1800s. Today that job is usually done by domestic cattle. The addition of barbed-wire fences to the plains has changed the way many birds see the landscape. Cattle are often carefully rotated between pastures. Because a single landowner makes decisions for their family's livelihood on acres bounded by fences, fire is often suppressed. However, in the case of the Flint Hills in eastern Kansas, fire is a social event for neighbors, and prescribed burning is deployed much more frequently than historic patterns. Today, eastern red-cedar and other wood species have crept into the fireless regions of the plains, changing the composition of the grassland bird communities to include more shrub and forest species. Time changes things, indeed.

Endemic Species of the Great Plains

Seventeen percent of the land area of North America is within the plains region. Oddly, relatively few birds have evolved in the grassland system—in fact, only 5 percent of North American birds evolved in prairies. We have already noted that grassland bird communities are simple, compared with the diverse groups of species found in forests with many niches available. So perhaps we would not expect as many species to come from grasslands because there are fewer niches.

As an example of this fairly simple system, my graduate student and her technicians counted over eight thousand individual birds in a large set of repeated surveys in upland pastures on eleven ranches in the Nebraska Sandhills during a recent summer. The research crew only counted in wide-open grasslands, avoiding areas near trees or wetlands; the total species count was fifty-two. A closer look at the results show that the two most common species, western meadowlark and grasshopper sparrow, accounted for 48 percent of the sightings. Brown-headed cowbird and lark sparrow combined to account for another 19 percent of the observations, so four species were written down as 67 percent of the observations on our survey sheets. Ten species accounted for 90 percent of our observations of grassland birds.

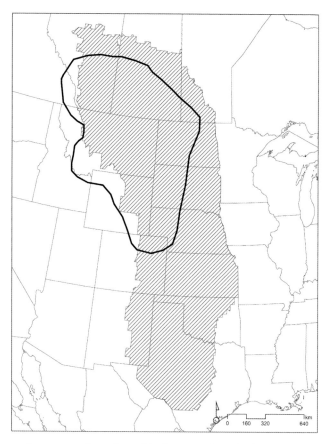

18. Approximate boundary of the hotspot where the distribution of at least four endemic prairie birds can be found (*dark outline*) relative to the Great Plains region (*hashed area*). After depictions by R. M. Mengel, "The North American Central Plains as an Isolating Agent in Bird Speciation," in *Pleistocene and Recent Environments of the Central Great Plains*, ed. W. Dort and J. K. Jones (Lawrence: University of Kansas Press, 1970), 279–340; and by F. L. Knopf, "Prairie Legacies—Birds," in *Prairie Conservation: Preserving North America's Most Endangered Ecosystem*, ed. F. B. Sampson and F. L. Knopf (Washington DC: Island Press, 1996), 135–48.

Endemic and near-endemic grassland species of the Great Plains, including passerines (songbirds) and nonpasserines*

	Passerines	Nonpasserines
Primary Endemics	Sprague's pipit	Mountain plover
	Cassin's sparrow	Long-billed curlew
	Baird's sparrow	Ferruginous hawk
	Lark bunting	
	McCown's longspur	
	Chestnut-collared longspur	
Near-endemics	Horned lark	Greater prairie-chicken
	Eastern meadowlark	Lesser prairie-chicken
	Western meadowlark	Sharp-tailed grouse
	Dickcissel	Upland sandpiper
	Savannah sparrow	Burrowing owl
	Grasshopper sparrow	Short-eared owl
	Henslow's sparrow	Mississippi kite
	Vesper sparrow	Northern harrier
	Lark sparrow	Swainson's hawk
	Clay-colored sparrow	Prairie falcon

*After lists compiled by the late Fritz Knopf, an ornithologist who worked with prairie birds his entire life.

Other researchers have reported similar results in the northern and southern Plains. Less than one hundred miles away, another member of my research team counted seventy-eight species of birds in her surveys of the mixed grassland and forest of the Niobrara River valley in northern Nebraska. Their top four species—house wren, spotted towhee, ovenbird, and red-eyed vireo—accounted for only 38 percent of their observations, and it took twenty-five species to hit the 90 percent mark in this wooded habitat that apparently had more niches, more bird species, and a more even distribution of the number of individuals in each species counted.

Not only are grasslands of the plains simple systems, but they are geologically young. The plains were covered by water while other areas of North America were fostering land-based animals. In addition, the plains were disturbed by glaciation multiple times, which changed the conditions under which animals were adapting to the plains region.

To gain insights into an ecosystem, biologists often turn to species of animals that are only found in that region, referred to as *endemic species*. We can think of endemic species as flag bearers for a region—its native sons and daughters. In the Great Plains, the epicenter for evolution of endemic species seems to be the shortgrass prairies of north-central Montana (figure 18). The northern plains have more endemics than the southern plains, and the short list of prairie-evolved birds (see table) paints a picture of the Great Plains as a region in which more bird species invade from the outside than evolve and spread from the inside. Forest- and shrub-dwelling species to the east or west find their way into suitable patches on the prairie. Waterbirds migrate through the plains from other regions, but no waterbirds are strictly plains-only birds.

There are six species of grassland songbirds, or passerines (the perching birds), that are endemic to the Great Plains. Four of the six are found in a small region in the northern Great Plains extending from the western Dakotas, northern Wyoming and Montana, and into the Canadian prairies. If you are looking for endemics, a trip to the northern plains would be prudent.

Baird's sparrow (figure 19) was discovered and named by John J. Audubon, in 1843, in North Dakota. It migrates to northern Mexico for the winter, and the species breeds only in the northern plains. Their populations shift each year in response to dynamic food resources. In fact, no one spotted another Baird's sparrow, with its proud set of streaks in the upper breast, for thirty years after Audubon first described it. Audubon did his work when the only way to adequately draw, color, and scientifically describe birds was to shoot a specimen (with fine shot to avoid destroying the complex features).

The chestnut-collared longspur (figure 19) is restricted to the northern plains during the breeding season, and it seeks out sparse habitat that has been grazed or mowed—a reflection of its interaction with bison over thousands of generations. The longspur teaches a valuable lesson for visitors to the plains: good habitat does not mean untouched habitat. Fires, grazing, and disturbance by burrowing animals like prairie dogs are natural and important for many birds. Removing any or all of these disturbances from an ecosystem can radically change it to the point that species start to disappear as the vegetation grows denser. McCown's longspur (figure 19) also prefers spare habitats and is found in the northern plains. The males establish territories with aerial displays, flying into the sky and singing while floating downward. If you are not impressed by this behavior, you may need to spend more time watching it.

The male lark bunting (figure 19) is a dapper fellow with his suit of black adorned with white patches on the wings. The species is found in the northern plains' hotspot for endemics, but also can be found as far south as western Kansas in the

19. Endemic species of the Great Plains. *From top, left to right*: Baird's sparrow (Rick Bohn, USFWS), chestnut-collared longspur (Rick Bohn, USFWS), McCown's longspur (Ron Knight, CCL), lark bunting (Alan Schmierer, CCL), Sprague's pipit (Gary Leavens, CCL), and Cassin's sparrow (Alan Schmierer, CCL).

southern plains. Like most of the smaller songbirds in the Great Plains, the male and female are present to defend the nest and take care of the nestlings and fledglings. Typically, one will stay at or near the nest while the other forages for food. If you find a nest in a grassland and then find a suitable viewing location that allows the birds to operate as if you were not there, you will be amazed at the number of flights that parents take after nestlings are hatched and gaping mouths need to be filled. A biologist at Pawnee National Grasslands in eastern Colorado found that a pair of lark buntings gathered most of the food for their nestlings within one hundred feet of their nest. Over half of the food items brought to the young were grasshoppers. When nestlings had just hatched, only one or two feeding trips were required each hour, but as the nestlings grew larger and more demanding of their parents, the foraging trips increased to almost twelve per hour. That is almost as many trips as I made to the grocery store to keep milk in the house when our son was a teenager.

The breeding grounds of Sprague's pipit (figure 19) are confined to the northern plains. Males spend long periods of time—up to a couple hours in some cases—engaged in their aerial displays to maintain the boundaries of their territory. Their eyes and bill look large, relative to the size of their head. Male Cassin's sparrows (figure 19) also engage in aerial displays during the breeding season, and the species is the sole representative of the southern plains on the list of small endemic birds. Cassin's sparrows may be more easily identified by what field marks they do not have, rather than those they do. Their head is generally plain with only a faint eye line, the chest is plain, and the wings lack dark or light bars.

We have already detailed the behaviors of the greater prairie-chicken (figure 20), and this prairie grouse is not explicitly an endemic of the Great Plains. Originally, the species was found east into the tallgrass prairies. However, corn and soybeans

20. Endemic species of the Great Plains. *From top*: greater prairie-chicken (Ethan Freese), long-billed curlew (unknown photographer), and mountain plover (Ron Knight, CCL).

have replaced critical habitat throughout Wisconsin, Illinois, and Iowa, and the core populations of prairie-chickens are now restricted to the central and northern Great Plains. Prairie-chickens were a part of the fabric of history of the Great Plains, as other stories in this book indicate. The lesser prairie-chicken and Attwater's prairie-chicken (figure 31) can also claim near-endemic status in the southern plains, and we will return to these two species when we discuss species of conservation concern.

The various species of prairie grouse (the prairie-chickens, sharp-tailed grouse, and greater sage-grouse) of the Great Plains are all members of the same order of birds, Galliformes, as the domestic chicken, and I have a personal bias toward all chick-enlike birds on the prairie. During the Civil War, one of my Powell ancestors was a blacksmith with Sherman's army as they swept a path through Georgia to the sea. One day, the story goes, the blacksmith was out foraging for food with a group of Yankee soldiers, when the Confederates surprised them. My ancestor took a bullet in the chest and started to bleed all over the place. He was taken back to camp, and in one of the few humorous stories of the Civil War, the doctor reported to him that he had not been shot. Instead, the shot had hit a chicken that he had scavenged and tucked into his coat. He had been shot in the chicken, and he survived to continue the line of Powells that led to me. You could say I owe everything to that chicken, and this may explain my research interests of ring-necked pheasants and greater prairie-chickens.

The unique bill of the long-billed curlew (figure 20) may be most useful on the wintering grounds where they look for inver-tebrates in the mud of wetlands along Mexico's coast. Curlews are known for dive-bombing anything that comes near their nest site, and the sheer calculation of mass of body size combined with the speed of their flight is enough to cause an interloping human visitor to quickly revisit calculations from high school physics regarding expected force of impact. My advice would be to duck and reverse course. Curlews arrive early to the plains in the spring and leave for their wintering grounds in June or early July while other species are in the midst of their breeding season. Do not expect to see curlews during a late-summer trip.

The western shortgrass prairie of the Great Plains is home to the mountain plover (figure 20). The species is another of the endemic species that uses sparse habitats, and they are often associated with prairie dog towns or lands heavily grazed by cattle. This rather plain-looking plover is misnamed, as they are not found near mountains. Mountain plovers are one of only a few species of birds with a rapid, multiclutch mating system. The female of a pair lays two clutches of eggs; the male incubates the first clutch, and the female incubates the second. Biologists have determined that nests tended by males have a better chance of producing chicks than those tended by females. Interestingly, once the chicks hatch, the new fledglings have a better chance of surviving if they are tended by the female, the opposite of the trend for nest survival.

Migration

The migratory birds of North America travel along aerial highways, called *flyways* by wildlife biologists (figure 21). The Pacific and Atlantic Flyways hug the coastlines, which provide sites for stopovers and cues for navigation. The Mississippi Flyway follows the largest north-south river in North America, the Mississippi River, which also offers a dependable source of water and a vertical path across the continent. In contrast, the Central Flyway has no north-south geographic feature for birds to use as a guide during migration. Not only is the Central Flyway lacking a visual map for birds, the flyway plows through the heart of the Great Plains, which is defined by its frequent droughts. Indeed, one could feel sorry for birds headed north

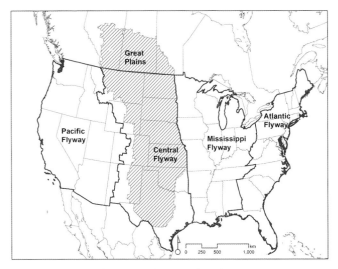

21. Four migratory flyways used to classify and manage migrating birds in North America. The Great Plains region (*hashed*) is within the borders of the Central Flyway.

or south over the plains with few landmarks to guide them and the potential for dry ponds and empty wetlands to greet them along their journey.

As a young graduate student at Iowa State University, I explored the idea that the choice of flyway might adversely affect mallard ducks migrating through the Central Flyway. I used the time patterns of recoveries of metal leg bands, attached to ducks by biologists in the north and recovered by hunters as ducks flew south, to compare the survival of mallards using the Mississippi Flyway with those using the Central Flyway. My advisers and I surmised that survival of mallards using the Mississippi River would be higher than survival of ducks migrating through the plains because a series of locks and dams keep water levels consistent on the Mississippi. The ducks knew the answer before we started our analysis, and we did not find any evidence for lower survival in the Central Flyway. My respect for those sturdy plains migrants received a booster shot, as it was clear that these mallards had found strategies to withstand what would seem to be relatively less favorable conditions, compared to the experience of their peers using other flyways.

If you are in the Great Plains during the spring or fall, it is a perfect time to join migrants at their stopover locations, areas where birds stop for resting and refueling of energy stores. Migration is a demanding activity, and different groups of birds have adopted their own strategies and timing for migration (figure 22). Typically, waterfowl start to move north earlier than other birds, and the ducks and geese also tend to stay north longer than other birds, completing their southward migration later in the year. Migration can be viewed as a big dice roll—the birds are taking a chance when they head north from their warmer wintering grounds. Will it be warm in the north when they arrive? Will food be available? Evidence suggests that waterfowl view that dice roll as less risky—their larger body sizes can buffer against cooler temperatures and short-term lack of food that might kill smaller birds.

The shorebirds—the plovers, sandpipers, snipes, and curlews—migrate next, as they need to wait for warm weather to unveil water and mud flats for foraging during migration. For shorebirds, it is early in and early out, as they are the first migrants to leave the breeding grounds to head south to beaches and coastal wetlands. It is possible they are trying to beat the human tourists to those destinations, but more likely they are concerned about food supply. For species of birds that find their food in mud and wet sand along lakes, ponds, and rivers, late-summer heat or the good chance for a drought on the plains has the potential to turn their smorgasbord into a food desert.

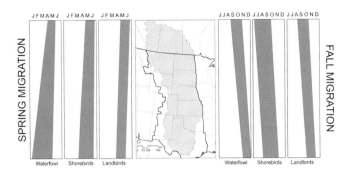

22. Migration chronology of waterfowl, shorebirds, and landbirds in the Central Flyway through the Great Plains (*hatched area*) during spring and fall migration. The range of dates represented by the *shaded bars* depict main migration times for each type of bird, for the southern, northern (United States), and northern (Canada) areas of the Great Plains.

The landbirds are the latest group to migrate north, and this group includes raptors and songbirds.

Why do some birds migrate? This question has been contemplated for centuries. In fact, Aristotle suggested in 350 B C in *Historia Animalium* that birds leave "the cold countries after the autumnal equinox to avoid the approaching winter, and after the spring equinox [migrate] from warm lands to cool lands to avoid the coming heat."

Aristotle was on the right track. We know that all animals have developed behavioral strategies to enhance their survival and reproduction. Birds migrate for the very same reasons: to stay alive and to enhance the numbers of baby birds they can provide to the world; and these young birds become the next generation.

The central and northern portions of the Great Plains are in the North American temperate region, where temperatures vary greatly between winter and summer months. Winters on the northern plains are renowned for thick ice on lakes and bitter blizzards, which blanket and trap food resources for birds. The warm temperatures and longer days of spring bring open waters, new plant growth, and a massive flush of aquatic and land-based insects, which serve as resources that birds can use to stay alive and breed. Therefore, we observe many bird species making an annual trek north and south in response to those resources.

Many migration journeys are spectacular in length. Radio-tracking devices show that some sandhill cranes journey from northern Mexico or the Texas coast through the Great Plains and Canada into Siberia to breed. Snow geese travel over three thousand miles from the southern plains to nest in the tundra around Hudson Bay and farther north. Blue-winged teal leave the breeding grounds of the northern prairies earlier than most waterfowl to reach their winter home more than seven thousand miles away in Argentina. Biologists believe that many of these long migrations started as shorter, seasonal shifts that grew gradually over thousands of years. Remember, we earlier noted that blue-winged teal show up in a Nebraska fossil record from 2 million years ago. Birds have adapted their migration routes to continental changes in climate as glaciers ground their way south across former avian breeding grounds. Migrants then shifted slowly northward as glaciers retreated to the north, unveiling new breeding areas. Geologists estimate that there have been over twenty glacial events during the last 2.5 million years. Bird migration is not a recent occurrence, and the current routes will undoubtedly change in the future.

Biologists wrestle with a key question as they attempt to understand how birds develop migratory behaviors: was migration a response to travel south by birds that called the north home, or was it a response to travel north by birds that called the south home? Should we view migration as a way for birds in the south to exploit temporary summer food resources in the north, or is migration a way for birds in the north to survive the winter? Recent evaluation of the family connections of songbird species suggests that it has been much more common for northern birds to shift their wintering grounds to the south. Therefore, the cheerful, bright spring warblers that we find migrating through the Great Plains are coming home. No wonder their songs are so beautiful.

Watching migration in action is a wonderful experience. I think migration is even more wonderful to watch as we consider the factors that motivate avian decisions that cause the movements we observe across our landscapes. For migratory species of birds, migration is hard-wired, a part of their internal clock. If a migratory bird is captured and taken indoors to a holding pen with lighting that changes to match the shortening days in the fall, the bird will become restless—pacing or fluttering about the pen—as its peers are starting to gather for migration in the wild. The behavior is known by the German word *zugunruhe*, meaning migratory restlessness. Across millions of years, migratory birds have responded to changes in the season to fill the skies as they fly south, leaving resident species of birds behind to prove their merit during harsh winters on the plains.

Sandhill cranes (figure 23) winter in northern Mexico, southern New Mexico, and Texas, making extensive use of wetlands and surrounding farm fields. Spring finds them making a journey northward with whole-flock pit stops in Kansas and Nebraska that are routinely featured on outdoor channels on cable television. Most cranes spend two to three weeks in the Platte River valley of Nebraska, and biologists consider the spectacle to be one of the most interesting migration events of any species on earth. When the sandhill cranes arrive at their breeding grounds in the north, there is a not-so-small chance that the ground will still be frozen. Therefore, the fat reserves accumulated along the Platte are essential for survival of the first couple of weeks on the breeding grounds, especially for the female cranes who are spending energy on creation of their eggs. Two subspecies, the greater and lesser, can be spotted in the Great Plains by looking for differences in height. Cranes typically reach cruising altitude for migratory flights at about a mile high, or five thousand feet, and it is common to hear them call to each other as they pass overhead before you see them.

Look at a flock of snow geese (figure 23) carefully to spot individuals with white or gray/blue color phases of plumage. Genetics control the color phase: like red hair in humans, the white color phase is a homozygous recessive trait, which means that both parents must contribute the right genetic material to make the white phase occur. Although the odds of that random combination are low, the white phase is common because young snow geese typically select a mate of the same color phase as their parents. One of the most exciting sights to be seen during spring migration in the plains is a large cyclone of circling snow geese preparing to land on pond or lake. The snow goose is a symbol of the effects of humans on the Great Plains. An abundance of corn in fields, spilled from combines during harvest, has contributed to very good body condition when snow geese reach the tundra to breed. The vegetation at their breeding colonies is often depleted by the superabundant populations, which has led wildlife managers to implement the only spring hunting season for waterfowl in North America to try to control numbers before the population crashes due to disease or lack of food on the breeding grounds. Spoiler alert: it has not worked.

The American avocet (figure 23) is an elegant bird with an upturned bill that it uses to forage for aquatic insects in shallow waters. Avocets in the plains migrate south to the Gulf Coast and farther south to the central valleys of Mexico and Central America. They are common migrants in the western plains, and they rely heavily on wetlands and shallow water bodies for

23. Migratory species of the Great Plains. (*From top*): sandhill crane (Manjith Kainickara, C C L), snow goose (Jessica Bolser, U S F W S), and American avocet (Joel Jorgensen).

food during their breeding season. Droughts may cause them to make local shifts to find food.

The mallard (figure 24) is the most common duck in North America. The green head of the male is a classic feature making for easy identification of the species. Mallards pair up each year in late fall and during the winter, and the male often follows the female to the nesting ground that she calls home. Mallards migrate from the southern U.S. to the northern U.S. and Canada, and migrations are fairly quick. They have been clocked at fifty-five miles per hour during migration, and typically are pushed south from the breeding grounds by weather systems that provide tailwinds. In urban settings, even to the north, some mallards may be seen year-round if ponds or rivers remain free of ice.

The canvasback (figure 24) is a duck species of conservation concern. The bird has a stately appearance with its longer bill, but the fact that it also tastes good caused it to be overhunted during market hunting days on the plains. A two-thousand-year-old canvasback decoy, used by hunters to lure birds within striking distance, was found in a cave in Nevada, which suggests people have been hunting canvasbacks for a long time. In the Atlantic Flyway, canvasbacks appear to have shifted their migration route to avoid the Chesapeake Bay as the water quality in the bay degraded and affected the availability of food. In the plains, canvasbacks nest in clumps of vegetation over open water. The species prefers deeper ponds and wetlands for nesting. Rather than expend energy for nesting in years of drought that may cause chicks to die, canvasbacks may delay or skip nesting, which has led to their smaller population size.

There are many reasons to fall in love with the Wilson's phalarope (figure 24). During migration, you may be lucky enough to find groups in small ponds and wetlands in the plains. If you look closely, you will notice the birds are spinning

24. Migratory species of the Great Plains. *From top*: mallard (Tom Koerner, U S F W S), canvasback (unknown photographer), and Wilson's phalarope, male *on left* and female *on right* (Tom Koerner, U S F W S).

about—as if one of their paddling legs was broken. The spinning is purposeful, as it is a way for the birds to concentrate aquatic insects and forage more efficiently. Phalaropes are also an example of one of the few species in which the traditional male and female roles are switched. The females lay eggs for at least one male and then disappear while the males guard and incubate each nest. The mating system is called polyandry (from Greek for "many men"), the opposite of polygyny ("many women"), and a form of polygamy (more than one mate). To complete the story, the female phalarope is more colorful than the male—again, the opposite of the coloration pattern of most bird species. It is dangerous work to sit on a nest with predators lurking in the landscape, and it is energetically demanding to produce eggs and care for young. For species in which females tend the nest alone, females tend to die at higher rates than males. Therefore, it is common for males to be colorful to assist them in competing for a smaller number of females. In phalaropes, we see the opposite dynamic, which confirms that the sex that has to be most competitive is also the sex most likely to be colorful.

A House Divided

Many identification books for North American birds are sold as two versions: one for eastern birds and one for western birds—two guides for two regions of the continent. That division of the continent harkens back to our earlier discussion of the formation of the Great Plains. The great inland sea that split the continent 85 million years ago causes us to ponder the processes that led to unique sets of species of animals in the west and east. Birds were evolving as the sea slowly dried and turned to wetlands, eventually making way for the grasslands of the modern Great Plains. Throughout this history, the unique nature of the Great Plains—an inland sea that became a continental valley between western and eastern mountain ranges—has served to separate, to some extent, the eastern and western birds (figure 25).

Since the last glaciation 10,000 years ago, the grasslands of the plains have served as a barrier to forest species from the west coming east, and vice versa. Intriguingly, as we compare the species in the west and east, we find several sister species, such as western and eastern meadowlark or Bullock's oriole and Baltimore oriole. Many of these species pairs are so closely related that ornithologists (the ones who spend time collecting samples of tissue and lurking about in laboratories with genetics equipment) constantly argue whether a pair represents two species, two subspecies, or two color forms of the same species. As with many things in life, once it is resolved, we tend to wait twenty to thirty years to bring up the same issue again and reverse our previous decision. In fact, by the time you read this book, it is possible that some species distinctions will have changed from the way they are presented here.

An early hypothesis to explain the presence of these sister species was based on the last glaciation event of some 10,000 years ago, which many call the late Pleistocene glaciation. Humans had arrived in the Great Plains before this glaciation event, and the infamous extinction of the megafauna, the large mammoths, ground sloths, and saber-toothed cats, occurred at the end of the Ice Age. Scientists surmised that the glacier physically separated individuals of the ancestor to the sister species of birds. The cold climate and other landscape changes that occurred during the Ice Age further separated individuals into two distinct subpopulations in eastern and western North America, according to this school of thought. When the glacier retreated, the birds on either side had changed slightly through many years of adapting to distinct habitats in the west and east; and so, the hypothesis suggested, sister species appeared. The suggestion made sense, but research has now largely proven it to be wrong.

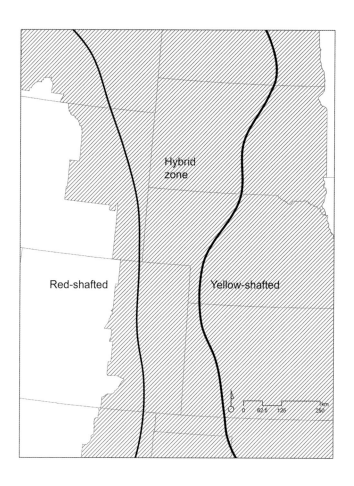

Red-shafted

Hybrid zone

Yellow-shafted

25. Approximate boundaries of the hybrid zone in the Great Plains for red-shafted and yellow-shafted forms of the northern flicker. Within the boundaries shown here, hybrids are more likely to be observed than elsewhere. After a map by T. A. Grudzien et al., "Genic population structure and gene flow in the Northern Flicker (*Colaptes auratus*) hybrid zone," *The Auk* 104, no. 4 (1987): 654–64.

Genetic analysis of pairs of species, such as the ones detailed below, suggests that sister pairs have a much longer history than just 10,000 years—in fact, most of the pairs have been singing different songs and sporting different plumage characteristics for 2 to 5 million years. Glaciation events that ushered in the start of the Pleistocene 2.5 million years ago may have contributed to the gradual divergence between some sister species, but species such as blue and Stellar's jays diverged over 5 million years ago. Their songs may have been over 2 million years old by the time the first, large glaciers advanced southward 2.5 million years ago.

Most of these sister pairs overlap at some point in the Great Plains, which makes bird watching in the plains a unique experience—you can find locations where both of the species pair sit on the same fence or sing from the same bush. For example, western and eastern kingbirds can be seen together in western Nebraska and South Dakota. Many of the pairs of species are known to interbreed, resulting in hybrids that are recognizable in some fashion—showing plumage or song characteristics of both species. Meadowlark hybrids, for example, often have a song that is a garbled mixture of the two species-specific songs. Other pairs of sister species tend to stay apart and not hybridize, so for these species we refer to this zone of overlap as a tension zone rather than a hybrid zone.

The dynamics of the interactions between the two species continue to change, even in the short amount of time that modern ornithologists have been focused on this issue in the last century. Immigrants to the plains planted trees, allowing forest- and shrub-dwelling birds to change their ranges and go deeper into the prairie region. Cities, with their abundant trees, formed islands of forest that could serve as stepping stones for forest species.

Western kingbirds and eastern kingbirds can both be found throughout the entire Great Plains (figure 26), especially as the western kingbird has expanded to the east due to tree planting. They are flycatchers, and it is fun to watch individuals hawking insects by flitting out from a perch to grab a bite in midair. Each species is found more frequently in their respective western and eastern regions, and they rarely hybridize.

The northern flicker has two forms: red-shafted in the west and yellow-shafted in the east (figure 26). The names for the two forms describe the color of the feather shafts of the wing and tail, which may be difficult to see without asking them to raise their wing to let you take a peek. This ground-foraging, large woodpecker was once considered two separate species, but it extensively hybridizes in a zone the splits the Great Plains and continues north and then west into Alaska.

Lazuli buntings and indigo buntings, both named after their blue plumage (figure 26), may have diverged as separate species over 3 million years ago. The lazuli, with its rosy breast and white belly, breeds from the Pacific coast east to the Great Plains, and the pure-blue indigo breeds from the Atlantic coast west to the Great Plains. The overlap in their ranges is four hundred to five hundred miles in width, and there are common reports of hybrids. Early ornithologists developed scoring systems to indicate the degree to which "how indigo" or "how lazuli" a specimen appeared as they investigated the hybrid zone in the plains.

Relative newcomers as sister species, spotted towhees and eastern towhees diverged only 400,000 years ago according to genetic tests (figure 27). They interbreed commonly in their small region of overlap on the plains and were once considered one species. As a reminder of their connection, both species have a three-note "drink-your-tea" song, but the spotted towhee's version is quicker and simpler (perhaps more like a tired parent frustrated with a child) than the more melodious, grandmotherly reminder from the eastern towhee.

26. Species of the Great Plains hybrid zone. Western birds are on *left*, eastern birds on *right*. *From top, left to right*) western kingbird (Becky Matsubara, CCL); eastern kingbird (Caleb Putnam, CCL); northern flicker, red-shafted form (Tom Koerner, USFWS); northern flicker, yellow-shafted form (Beth Fishkind); lazuli bunting (Don Owens, CCL); and indigo bunting (Jim Hudgins, CCL).

27. Species of the Great Plains hybrid zone. Western birds are on *left*, eastern birds on *right*. *From top, left to right*: spotted towhee (Becky Matsubara, CCL), eastern towhee (Kelly Colgan Azar, CCL), western meadowlark (Becky Matsubara, CCL), eastern meadowlark (Jim Hudgins, USFWS), Bullock's oriole (Alan Schmierer, CCL), and Baltimore oriole (unknown photographer).

Western meadowlarks and eastern meadowlarks diverged 2.6 million years ago, and their vocalizations are the best way to tell them apart (figure 27). Eastern meadowlarks may have a mostly white moustache stripe trailing from the bill, while westerns have a bit of yellow in that stripe. Although the species are almost identical in description, they hybridize very rarely, which may emphasize the importance of song in breeding decisions. The western meadowlark's range extends east from the Pacific coast through the Great Plains to Illinois and Michigan, and it is the state bird of five Great Plains states (North Dakota, Nebraska, Kansas, Montana, and Wyoming) and Oregon. The eastern meadowlark's range comes from the Atlantic coast into the eastern portion of the central and southern plains. Not a single state selected the eastern meadowlark as the state bird, which has to be embarrassing.

Bullock's orioles and Baltimore orioles (figure 27) provide a classic example of how tenuous decisions can be ("Yes they are," "No they aren't," "Yes they are") in conferring separate species status. In my lifetime, they have been lumped from two species together into the northern oriole and then split again into two species. The two orioles hybridize extensively in the Great Plains, which leads to the taxonomic arguments. Human modification of the Great Plains has changed the dynamics of their hybridization as well. Baltimore orioles, with their all-black heads and dark wings, have moved westward in Nebraska, and the hybrid zone has shifted over one hundred miles westward in just twenty years. Just to the south, in Kansas, Bullock's oriole with its orange face and white wing patch has moved eastward, causing a similar eastward shift in the hybrid zone. Hybrid orioles have a mixture of characteristics such as all-black heads with white wing patches, and their presence makes birding in the Great Plains all the more interesting. The presence of sister species at opposite sides of the Great Plains is a reminder that evolution is a long, dynamic process. Pairs of species have separate histories and timelines, and the Great Plains has played a unique role as a fluctuating environment through repeated periods of avian invasions from west and east into the plains and glaciation events that forced populations apart. Depending on whether you are a glass-half-full or glass-half-empty kind of person, you may view these sister pairs as symbols of division caused by an empty grassland and ice, or you may view these species as evidence of genetic connections across the continent. Either way, the Great Plains provides a unique opportunity to observe the results of timeless breeding processes. One has to wonder if the lazuli bunting or Bullock's oriole, singing mightily from the top of a shrub along your trail, might sing with more pride if they could comprehend the weight of their history.

CHAPTER THREE

The Problems

Humans and Birds on the Plains

We should start with the good news. The Great Plains has a wealth of intact habitat for wildlife. Visually compare (in figure 28) the relative proportion of intact habitat in states in the Corn Belt (choose my birth state of Iowa for the most drastic comparison) to states in the Great Plains. It is obvious that agriculture crop production is relatively limited in many areas of the Great Plains—chiefly due to soil structure (rocky or sandy), topography (too much slope or poor drainage), and low precipitation levels. Intact habitat and the lack of row-crop agriculture is thus one reason that birds and other wildlife are more abundant in some regions in the Great Plains.

However, the relationship between birds and humans on the plains contains an uncomfortable history of landscape change, which is a story of lost opportunity for wildlife as well. To be honest with ourselves, it is important to tell the story from an informed perspective. We should avoid naïve chastisements of agriculture, the chief industry that has removed land from its natural status. Everyone has to make a living, and if you drive anywhere in the Great Plains it will be clear that the majority of the people in the region support their families with agriculture. If you are in the eastern plains or along rivers that allow irrigation, fields of corn and soybeans will surround you. Farther west, you will see wheat fields in drier country. On rocky or

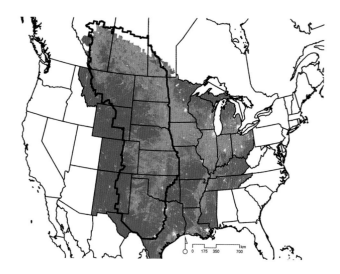

28. Status of landscapes in the central United States in 2015, overlaid with the Great Plains boundary, showing areas with intact (*green*) habitats (forest, grassland, wetland, etc.) and those areas converted to agriculture (*brown*). Cities and other development are *white*. Public data from World Wildlife Fund.

sandy soils, you will find grazing land for cattle. The towns that offer you a prime rib sandwich and a slice of homemade pie are arranged and built to operate as agricultural trade centers. Ag is king in the Great Plains. In 2016 the ten states in the Great Plains contributed 27 percent of agriculture production in the U.S. as measured by cash receipts; and the most central Great Plains states, Nebraska and Kansas, were ranked third and seventh among U.S. states in agriculture production.

Farmers feed us, so we need farms and ranches, and we need farmers and ranchers. The map of the Great Plains should not be expected to show completely intact habitats. Grain must be planted, and fields must be cleared. The key for the future is to make good decisions about land use from an efficiency standpoint and an ecosystem standpoint. A farmer in Namibia, in southern Africa, once commented to me that the fields around his home without birds would be like a home without a child. Our ecosystems must be productive, but we must also maintain the fabric that is the nature of the Great Plains.

The Great Plains has lost half of its grassland to agricultural production and tree invasions or plantings. In addition, states and provinces in the Great Plains have lost 35–65 percent of their wetlands (figure 29). In a relative sense, perhaps we in the plains should be grateful for what remains—to the east of the Great Plains, Iowa has lost 90 percent of its wetlands, and biologists scour old cemeteries to find prairie seeds as the graveyards are some of the only unplowed grasslands remaining in the state.

What does the loss of habitat mean for birds? The Breeding Bird Survey has been conducted each year since 1966 across the United States and Canada. The survey allows scientists to monitor trends in population numbers, which continue to suggest that grassland birds are some of the most imperiled birds on the continent. Declines in grassland birds are not surprising given the removal of grasslands that has occurred. In the central region of the continent, species of grassland birds show some of the largest declines in numbers during 1966–2015 compared to waterbirds or forest birds. McCown's longspur and chestnut-collared longspur, both Great Plains endemics, have declined by 6 percent and 4 percent per year. Sprague's pipit (another endemic), eastern meadowlark, lark bunting, horned lark, mountain plover (endemic), and northern bobwhite are down by 3 percent per year. Baird's sparrow (endemic), northern flicker, and grasshopper sparrow are down by 2 percent. Western meadowlark, eastern kingbird, and long-billed curlew are down by 1 percent. We might conclude that the greatest profession in the Great Plains is not that of an endemic grassland bird.

29. Cartoon by Jay N. "Ding" Darling, August 14, 1923. Courtesy of the Jay N. "Ding" Darling Wildlife Society and with permission of the University of Iowa Libraries, Special Collections Department.

To look at the declines across the fifty-year period of the Breeding Bird Survey, we have to use some accounting techniques to estimate the proportion of individuals left in the Great Plains—like calculating cumulative loss from several years of bad investments in the stock market. For the species with the smallest decline of 1 percent per year, the population size is only 61 percent of what it was 1966. A 2 percent decline per year: 36 percent are left. A 3 percent decline: 22 percent are left in 2015. It is remarkable, actually, and quite sad. Their future depends on better choices and innovative ideas to design productive farms with wildlife habitat in the Great Plains.

The story of habitat change in the Great Plains is the story of agriculture. As European and eastern American immigrants came to the plains, these homesteaders were distributed across the landscape to toil and improve their acres. They became farmers. As society entered the twentieth century, agriculture became a science. Breeding programs were established to create hybrid corn, which grew at higher densities and yielded more but required more nutrients (fertilizer). Wetlands were drained to put more land into production (figure 29). One of my favorite stories from Nebraska describes a family spending the entire winter creating a tunnel using shovels and a candle so that water from a wetland on their farm could be channeled under a bordering hill to the nearby river. Imagine the effort, spent with a high level of personal risk of injury or death in a tunnel like those dug by prison escapees, just to get a little more cropland into production. On farm after farm after farm across the Great Plains, small decisions were made that quickly transformed the landscape. By 1920 most states in the plains had converted the amount of cropland to agriculture that remains as cropland today.

There were hiccups along the way. Just prior to the Dust Bowl and Great Depression of the 1930s, farmers had pushed the crop acres to the highest point ever reached by attempting to farm land that should not have been tilled. The marginal lands were on slopes and poor soils, and the decision to plow too much came back to haunt many farmers in the form of wind and water erosion that occurred during the Dust Bowl years.

Mechanization came to the family farm, and tractors replaced horses. Farms and field sizes grew as one farmer with a tractor could do the job of two or more using horses. Synthetic fabrics replaced wool, and farmers bid good-bye to their sheep. Refrigeration meant that a milk cow was not needed on every farm, and numbers of milk cows followed the declines in sheep. Farms needed fewer pastures with no horses, sheep, or milk cows, so crop fields were enlarged. Without horses, oats were not needed, so the oat field was replaced with corn. By the 1960s, the family farm had larger fields and fewer livestock. You might also surmise they had fewer birds, because of the disappearance of pastures and small-grain fields. And you would be correct.

In the next fifty years, irrigation became more affordable and widespread. Sounds of the Dust Bowl still rang in farmers' ears, and irrigation was a way to avoid such a disaster in the future—a direct pipeline from the aquifer under their feet to their crops. In 1972 Nebraska had more irrigated crop acres than dryland (nonirrigated) crop acres for the first time. If you have flown over the Great Plains, you may have spotted our crop circles (figure 57), caused by the rotations of the center-pivot irrigation systems. To install a center-pivot system, a farmer needed to clear 160 acres, or one-fourth of a square mile. More wildlife habitat was removed as the incredible system was installed that made the farmer more immune to droughts that can ruin life and livelihood in the plains. As I like to remind my students, at each step of the way, people made decisions with the best of intentions—to feed their family, increase profits, and make use of current technology. And, along the way, the rural

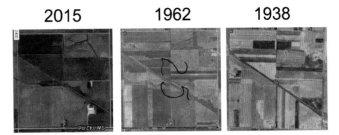

2015 **1962** **1938**

30. Changes in agricultural practices including loss of farmsteads, consolidation of fields, and fewer types of crops on a square mile in Saline County south of DeWitt, Nebraska, during 1938–2015. Photos from the Conservation Survey Division, University of Nebraska, prepared by Paige Krupa.

landscape changed. Socially, neighborhoods lost farm families as farms were consolidated (figure 30), and small towns became smaller. Grocery stores disappeared and along with them, wildlife was often marginalized in the process. No one meant to remove grocery stores and wildlife from the Great Plains, but it happened.

Today, the trend toward larger and fewer farms continues. Expansion of biofuels as a market for corn, along with remarkable breeding programs to make corn more immune to the effects of droughts and dry conditions, have pushed corn west into drier regions that once supported only sorghum or wheat. Unfortunately, corn is much less friendly for grassland birds than were the smaller grains it has replaced.

We also see an increased trend to plant crops in marginal areas with poor soil, harkening back to the mistakes made in the Dust Bowl. Ironically, the current agricultural policies that emerged during the droughts of the 1930s to support farmers and remove land from production now provide low-cost crop insurance that can cover losses when crops do not grow in these marginal lands. With those economic forces in place, it would be pure stupidity for a farmer not to plant crops anywhere they can. So we must pause to think about how farmers make decisions before criticizing them as they attempt to feed their families. Conservation efforts in grassland landscapes are dwarfed by powerful economic forces, and successful planning for the future must focus on ways to integrate native features into highly productive agricultural landscapes.

It is common for well-meaning citizens of the plains to complain about state wildlife agencies and their management of game birds. My response: during your next drive, stop your car on a hill and ask yourself, "Where would I be if I was a pheasant?" The hilltop reveals that over 95 percent of the landscape in the Great Plains is owned by private citizens—not managed by the state wildlife agency. And on that farmed landscape, there is very little wildlife cover left.

Not all species of wildlife have reacted negatively to agriculture in the plains. We have more deer and turkeys than ever before. Snow geese, noted earlier, have increased in numbers, as have sandhill cranes. All of these species have one thing in common: they have adapted well to the presence of corn fields.

Species of Conservation Concern

The greater sage-grouse (figure 31) is the largest of the prairie grouse on the plains and the species inhabits the western edge of the prairies where shortgrass prairie transitions to sage brush. A visit to a breeding display ground, or lek site, will provide a memorable opportunity to watch the males dance. In a show that would leave Dr. Seuss flabbergasted, their inflated yellow air sacs heave violently in a jiggling blanket of white breast feathers, while ornamental feathers on the tops of their heads stand on end and their tails spread in a magnificent sunburst. The birds are dependent on the sagebrush system, as they eat the leaves and buds during the winter and early spring when insects are no longer available. Sage-grouse have declined because of the removal of sagebrush to increase acres of grass for cattle. Ranchers do not make money from sagebrush. Profits to pay back the bank loan on the ranch come from beef production, and this is the heart of the problem—greater sage-grouse are at an economic disadvantage. To make matters worse, sagebrush country sits on top of oil and natural gas reserves, and energy development has pushed many sage-grouse from their former range. Conservation efforts have focused on how sage-grouse can coexist with energy development. A recent controversial decision by the U.S. Fish and Wildlife Service stated that sage-grouse conservation efforts had been successful enough to remove the species from consideration for listing as a threatened species. The world is watching to see if regional and state-level management efforts can support the species so that it does not need relisting at the federal level.

The lesser prairie-chicken (figure 31) on the southern plains is a smaller version of its northern cousin, the greater prairie-chicken (figure 20). Lesser prairie-chickens seem to be more sensitive to habitat fragmentation, energy development, and grazing. The species was listed as a threatened species by the U.S. Fish and Wildlife Service in 2014, but was removed from that status after a lawsuit. Many other endangered or threatened species can rely on public lands—national parks, national wildlife refuges, or national forests—for refuges and safe holds for recovery, but the southern plains is overwhelmingly affected by management by private individuals. Watch for news stories about this species, as well as more legal battles, which point to the dark side of conservation efforts. Shortsighted individuals see conservation of a single species to be of lower priority than the interests of agriculture and energy development. Creative people will find a way to enable both to exist.

31. Species of conservation concern in the Great Plains. *From top*: greater sage-grouse (Jennifer Stafford, USFWS), lesser prairie-chicken (USFWS), and Attwater's prairie-chicken (USFWS).

There is a single location in Texas, the Attwater Prairie Chicken National Wildlife Refuge, which is home to the only wild population of less than fifty individuals of the critically endangered Attwater's prairie-chicken (figure 31). This grouse is a close cousin (a subspecies) to the greater prairie-chicken of the northern plains. The species may have a namesake wildlife refuge, but it still struggles to reproduce as invasive fire ants can attack newly hatched chicks. A recovery program is attempting to raise birds in confinement and reintroduce them to the wild. The refuge is also in the path of hurricanes that frequent the Texas coastline and threaten to wipe out the entire population. The odds are stacked against survival of this species.

The interior population of the least tern (figure 33) was given endangered species status in 1985. They nest on bare sandbars along rivers in the Great Plains, and our rivers are not the rivers that Native Americans traversed just two centuries ago. Dams in rivers have raised water levels and removed the natural dynamics from floods that created sandbar nesting habitat. Hydroelectric plants along rivers withdraw water to generate power, but the water is stored in holding ponds until it is needed during peak hours of electrical demand each day. The result is that water is released through the power plant periodically, giving the downstream water levels an appearance of tidal conditions at a coastline (figure 32). Water levels rise and fall by almost two feet, which can render some sandbars unusable for nesting birds like the least tern who have no access to personal floatation devices. More extreme conditions are created from withdrawals of irrigation water from rivers in the plains, which can result in dry-river conditions during nesting season when combined with droughts. Least terns eat fish—males deliver fish to the female on the nest, and the pair feed fish to their chicks. It stands to reason that when the river dries up, the fish will dry up as well.

32. Representative daily changes in level of the Platte River near North Bend, Nebraska (gauge 06796000) just downstream from an outlet from a hydroelectric power plant as measured by a river gauge over seven days in July 2018. U S G S public data. Photo of nesting interior least terns by Jane Ledwin, U S F W S.

The piping plover (figure 33) is a sister species to the least tern—quite unrelated but bound by their love of the same nesting habitat. Piping plovers also nest on bare sandbars along rivers, and the birds were listed as an endangered species in 1985. Like least terns and Attwater's prairie-chicken, the piping plover's recovery depends on increasing the success of their nests. Biologists, anticipating floods, have developed a method to move nests to higher ground on a sandbar, and they found that the birds will follow their nest to higher ground and continue to nest. However, and this is the really interesting part, they are more likely to continue to nest if the larger rocks, branches, or other visually unique items that were in the immediate vicinity of their nest are moved and placed in similar locations around the new nest site. Home, sweet home.

33. Species of conservation concern in the Great Plains. *From top*: least tern (Ethan Freese), piping plover (Joel Jorgensen), and whooping crane in the middle of sandhill cranes (Ethan Freese).

Whooping cranes (figure 33) were one of the original species listed as endangered under the Endangered Species Act of 1973. In the 1940s only fourteen whooping cranes were living in the wild. These cranes signify many of the conservation problems of the early twentieth century—their white plumage made them a target of hunters (figure 34), and their dependence on wetlands during migration and on their wintering grounds on the coasts of Texas almost guaranteed their decline. For years, we did not know where whooping cranes were breeding—only that they headed north and disappeared until they reemerged during fall migration. However, in 1954, a forester who was flying to scout for fires spotted nesting pairs in Wood Buffalo National Park in Alberta, Canada, and whooping cranes continue to nest in this single region to this day. A significant captive rearing program has contributed to their wild numbers, and we have also learned a few lessons about captive rearing and conservation. For example, early efforts to raise whooping cranes involved taking eggs from wild nests and having sandhill cranes rear them in a captive facility—it turned out that the whooping crane chicks bonded with their foster parents and wanted nothing to do with whooping cranes of the opposite sex when it came to, well, you know. Now, chicks are fed (I kid you not) by men and women wearing a disguise that looks like a white HAZMAT suit or a super-sized beekeeper's suit. Food is delivered to newly hatched chicks with a puppetlike pincher device designed to look like a mama whooping crane. In 2006 a group of whooping cranes were raised in this manner and taught to fly behind an ultralight plane, piloted by a man wearing a whooping crane–like suit (see? ornithology can be great fun!). The ultralight led the cranes on a trip to Florida, where biologists wanted to establish a new population to reduce risk of extinction. Unfortunately, a tornado ripped through the holding facility in February of 2007, killing all of the whooping cranes that had been so carefully

34. A whooping-crane hunter. Photographed by S. Upton, near Elm Creek, Nebraska, in the 1890s. From the collection of Joel Sartore, used with permission.

prepped and delivered. The strategy continued, however, and several cranes have been added to this wild population in the last decade. When you think of conservation and recovery of bird species in the Great Plains, keep in mind the stalwart efforts and imagination of men and women who dedicate their lives to the protection and support of these critical species—men and women who have to depend on some successes to help them persevere through failures like the weather event that threatened to end the attempt to spread whooping cranes to Florida.

Birds and Society

Just a few years ago, I was talking to a rancher in the Sandhills region of Nebraska. Our research team was asking for permission to conduct surveys on his land to evaluate effects of cattle grazing on the diversity of the songbird community. We cannot do this type of research in the Great Plains without cooperation from landowners, and the conversation is always a bit of a dance: we ask politely, the rancher questions, in a somewhat bewildered fashion, why such counting of birds is worthwhile, we describe our study, the rancher asks if we intend to find any endangered species, and so it goes. Most landowners will eventually provide permission when they determine that our team is dependable and level-headed. The ranchers need to trust that we will shut gates to keep their cattle where they want them and that we will respect their property. Before we leave, they typically tell us a story about birds on their property.

On this early spring day, the rancher pointed to a bald eagle nest about a mile down the road from his house in a small stand of cottonwood trees that rose from the sea of grass. "You see that nest?" he asked. "Those eagles were adding sticks to that nest last fall, in October. I thought that was a little early to be worrying about their nest, so I kept watching them."

He continued, "Those cottonwood branches are really long and thick, and it is amazing that they can lift them, really. You can see them fly out and pick up a branch from where it is lying on the ground, and they work together as a pair."

We all nodded in agreement. Eagles are impressive, and their nests are simply huge structures. Bald eagles begin to incubate eggs in their nest as early as late February in the Great Plains. The species is a success story of environmental regulations to end use of DDT, a pesticide that affected the development of the shells of their eggs; the thin eggshells would break when the eagles incubated them. DDT was banned in the United States in 1972, and bald eagles were among the first species to be listed as an endangered species under the Endangered Species Act of 1973. In 1991 the first modern eagle nest to be found in Nebraska was discovered, and bald eagles were removed from the federal list of endangered and threatened species in 2007. There are now more than one hundred nests of bald eagles distributed throughout almost every corner of Nebraska, and one of them just happened to be the subject of our conversation.

"The next spring," the rancher noted, "I saw one of the eagles sitting on that nest, and I looked around at my pastures. The ground was still frozen, and all of the dead tree branches on the ground were completely iced down. And then I realized— those eagles knew that they had to add sticks to their nest in October, because they wouldn't be able to do it in late winter."

We grinned. The rancher was obviously very proud of his observation, and these little insights into nature's dynamics are what keep us going as research biologists as well.

The rancher arrived at the punch line. "So I went over and told my hired man that he needs to think more like an eagle: plan ahead and think about the future, not just what is happening at the moment. That is one smart bird."

As we drove down the long lane from the rancher's house through the grass-covered dunes of the Sandhills region, I thought about his story. People in the Great Plains have been watching and learning from birds for as long as there have been people in the Great Plains. We ask birds to tell us the story of the land around us, and we add chapters each day.

Native Americans

Birds were a source of food and inspiration to the first peoples in North America. Inspiration was translated into myth and legends—stories that were told in Native American communities to explain the unknown and to celebrate life. In the Great Plains in 1800, the Comanche lived in the current political regions of central-northern Texas and eastern New Mexico. They paid respect to the powerful eagle with their explanation of the eagle's creation. The story is told of a chief's young son who died, and the chief prayed in sorrow. The chief's son was transformed into the first eagle as an answer to his father's prayers, and the Comanche eagle dance celebrates this legend. The wearing of eagle feathers during the dance is considered a high honor, and the dancers often re-create the life cycle of the eagle with outstretched arms, often covered in feathers to symbolize the wings of the eagle. In modern times, only individuals with American Indian ancestry are legally allowed to obtain eagle feathers to continue these traditions.

Many tribes in North America believed the eagles could carry messages between the heavens and earth, and various names were assigned by tribes to the thunderbird, a mythical larger-than-life eagle, which was responsible for creating thunder and lightning by beating its wings.

Among the Pawnee—who in 1800 lived in the current political regions of central Nebraska and northern Kansas—the eagle was a symbol of fertility because of their large nests and their

35. Rushing Eagle, member of the Sioux nation, wearing buckskin clothing with a fur and bear-claw necklace and with a cloth on his head with three eagle feathers, taken 1870– 91. Library of Congress collection LC-USZ 62–131772, photographer unknown.

bold protection of the young eagles in the nest. The Pawnee also honored the eagle with songs, chants, and dance.

The greater prairie-chicken is a good-sized bird for a person looking for a meal, and Native Americans found these birds to be excellent eating. Early people were also impressed by the prairie-chicken's annual cycle of breeding, which consisted of males gathering in groups to dance with head-bobbing and strutting and jumping to compete for females and mating opportunities. The Teton Sioux, who in 1800 lived in the current political regions of western Nebraska, South Dakota, and North Dakota, and other tribes celebrate these unique behaviors with dance, and this legend explains why the Sioux honor prairie-chickens:

> There was a Sioux brave who went out to hunt to find food for his family. He was searching for deer or turkey, but wandered all day without finding any. As the day closed, he found a prairie-chicken. He did not want to kill the bird, because he knew it was small and it gave music to the plains. But, his family was hungry. So he decided to take the bird, so he could feed his family.
>
> That night, the prairie-chicken came to the man in his dreams. "I'm sorry to kill you," the man explained. "But my family was hungry."
>
> The bird replied that this was the way of the earth—to provide for your family. "But," the bird said, "You must now remember me."
>
> And so the Sioux people have always danced the dance of the prairie-chicken, to remember the sacrifice that the birds give to provide for the Sioux people.

Crows were revered by many tribes, and the birds were recognized for their intelligence and cunning. The Brulé Sioux, one of the groups that made up the Teton Sioux, observed that it was unusual for a bird to be black, with no color markings whatsoever. They developed this legend, told on the Rosebud Indian Reservation in South Dakota, as an explanation for why the crow is black:

In days long past, when the earth and the people on it were still young, all crows were white as snow. In those ancient times the people had neither horses nor firearms, and they depended upon the buffalo hunt for food.

The crow was the brother and friend of the buffalo, and he made the hunt difficult for the hunters by warning his buffalo friends: "Caw, caw, caw, hunters are coming."

The people were starving because crow had once again interfered with the hunt, and one wise old chief made this suggestion: "We must capture the big white crow and teach him a lesson. It is either that or go hungry."

The chief brought out a large buffalo skin, with the head and horns still attached. He put it on the back of a young brave, saying: "Nephew, sneak among the buffalo. They will think you are one of them, and you can capture the big white crow."

Disguised as a buffalo, the young man crept among the herd as if he were grazing. The big, shaggy beasts paid him no attention.

Then the hunters marched out from their camp after him, their bows at the ready. As they approached the herd, crow flew to warn the buffalo and he landed near the young man, who reached out and caught crow by the legs.

The people sat with the crow in their council, and the white bird was tethered with a rawhide and stones, so he could not escape. The people asked: "What shall we do with this big, bad crow, who has made us go hungry again and again?"

"I'll burn him up!" answered one angry hunter, and before anybody could stop him, he yanked the crow from the hands of his captor and thrust it into the council fire, string, stone and all. "This will teach you," he said.

The fire burned through the rawhide, and crow managed to fly out of the fire, but he was very badly singed and his feathers were charred black. He was no longer white. "Caw, caw, caw," he cried, flying away as quickly as he could, "I'll never do it again; I'll stop warning the buffalo, and so will my brother and sister crows. I promise! Caw, caw, caw."

Thus the crow escaped. But ever since, all crows have been black.

Native American folklore is rich with strong and strange characters, and none of the characters are as peculiar as Old-man. To groups such as the Blackfeet, who in 1800 lived in the current political region of west-central Montana, Old-man sometimes appears as a creator-god, and other times as a fool or a thief or a clownish character. Old-man occupies a position below that of the Great God, often known as Manitou. As such, Old-man is a unique combination of a fallible human being and an oft-powerful under-god. The Blackfoot legend for why the curlew's bill is long and crooked suggests that Old-man can make mistakes, and he is not to be trusted.

> One day in the springtime, Old-man saw some mice playing a game near a big flat rock near a creek. The sun had melted the frost from the earth about the rock, loosening it, so that it was about to fall. The Chief-Mouse would sing a song, while all the other mice danced, and then the chief would cry "now!" and all the mice would run past the big rock. On the other side, the Chief-Mouse would sing again, and then say "now!" And back they would come, right below the dangerous rock.
>
> Old-man said, "Chief-Mouse, I want to try that. I want to play that game. I am a good runner." Old-man said this

even though he was not a good runner, but he thought he was. That is often where we make great mistakes: when we try to do things we were not intended to do.

"No, no!" cried the Chief-Mouse, as Old-man prepared to make the race past the rock. "You will shake the ground, and you are too heavy. The rock may fall and kill you. My people are light of foot and fast. We are having a good time, but if you should try to do as we are doing you might get hurt, and that would spoil our fun."

Old-man replied, "Ho, stand back! I'll show you what a runner I am."

And Old-man ran. He ran like a grizzly bear, and shook the ground with his weight. Swow! The great rock fell on top of Old-man and held him fast in the mud, and Old-man screamed and called for aid. The Mice-people were too small to help Old-man, so they ran away to find help. Finally, they found the Coyote, and told him what had happened. Coyote didn't like Old-man very much, but he said he would go and see what he could do. The Mice-people showed him to the place where Old-man was still deep in the mud with the big rock on his back. Old-man was angry and was saying things people should not say, for they do no good and make the mind wicked.

Coyote said: "Keep still, you big baby. Quit kicking about so. You are splashing mud in my eyes. How can I see with my eyes full of mud? Tell me that. I am going to try to help you out of your trouble." But Old-man insulted Coyote by calling him a name that is not good, so the Coyote said, "Well, stay there!" and went away.

Again Old-man began to call for helpers, and the Curlew, who was flying over, saw the trouble, and came down to the ground to help. In those days Curlew had a short, stubby bill, and he thought that he could break the rock by pecking it. He pecked and pecked away without making any headway, until Old-man grew angry at him, as he did at the Coyote. The harder the Curlew worked, the worse Old-man scolded him. Old-man lost his temper altogether, which is a bad thing to do as it causes us to lose our friends. Temper is like a bad dog about a lodge: no friends will come to see us when he is about.

Curlew did his best but finally said: "I'll go and try to find somebody else to help you. I guess I am too small and weak. I shall come back to you." He was standing close to Old-man when he spoke, and Old-man reached out and grabbed the Curlew by the bill. Curlew began to scream, "Oh my, oh my, oh my" as you still hear them in the air when it is morning. Old-man hung onto the bill and finally pulled it out long and slim, and bent it downward, as it is today. Then he let go and laughed at the Curlew.

"You are a queer-looking bird now. That is a homely bill, but you shall always wear it and so shall all of your children, as long as there are Curlews in the world."

The world has forgotten who it was that got Old-man out of his trouble and from under the rock, but it is possible it was the bear.

On the Trail

Several explorers from Europe or the eastern U.S. traversed the Great Plains in the seventeenth and eighteenth centuries. Perhaps the most significant step in the expansion of the United States into the Great Plains was the well-documented journey of Meriwether Lewis and William Clark up the Missouri River during 1805 to 1806. This famous expedition provided definition to an unknown region of the expanding United States of America, and Lewis and Clark also documented a variety of

36. Long-billed curlew in flight. Photo by L. Bush, USFWS.

birds during their journey. Among the species first described by the expedition were the least tern and greater sage-grouse, both of which are now flirting with endangered species status. These birds and their habitats were largely a well-kept secret until Lewis and Clark made their detailed reports back to President Jefferson, and the rigors of their journey served to suggest that the Rocky Mountains were still a formidable barrier for westward travel.

Following Lewis and Clark, the deeper Missouri River provided a transport system for heavy bison furs in the northern Great Plains, which were fairly easy to float down the Missouri toward St. Louis. Fur traders had been using the shallow, braided rivers of the central plains, such as the Platte and the Kansas, as a route for accessing furs from smaller mammals such as beaver, which could be transported back by wagon or shallow-drafted keelboats. Beavers, the architects of local ecosystems with their energetically built dams, had been trapped, stacked, stretched, and transported from the Great Plains by 1830, so fur trappers headed deeper into the Rocky Mountain region. If you dare to call the Great Plains "flyover country" today, your feelings were first expressed by early fur traders who were headed for the Rockies. These early travelers also considered the plains a place to survive before they reached their destination. Most probably agreed with Major Stephen Long, who wrote the following as he left his exploration of the Rocky Mountains in 1820 to head back east along the Arkansas River: "More than one thousand miles of dreary and monotonous plain lay between us and the enjoyments and indulgences of civilized countries."

The valleys of the west-to-east rivers of the Great Plains became efficient transport routes from Iowa and Missouri as traders, explorers, and others began to extend the reach of eastern populations. In 1823 the far west was opened when a merchant from St. Louis, named William Henry Ashley, found the South Pass in southwestern Wyoming that allowed easier access across the Rocky Mountains. The valley of the Platte River was a logical east-west route to the South Pass.

Traders who took goods to Mexico used the Santa Fe Trail and passed through the Arkansas and Cimarron to reach Santa Fe from Independence, Missouri, for sixty years beginning in the 1820s. Explorers, fur trappers, farmers, and traders used the Oregon Trail through the Platte River valley to reach the Rockies on their way to the Pacific Northwest. The trail was accessible only on horseback early in the nineteenth century until the first wagon trains cleared the trail in 1836. Nearly half a million settlers would eventually pass along the trail, including forty thousand Mormons headed to Salt Lake City, Utah, between 1847 and 1860. Over one hundred thousand miners and associated traders used the Oregon route to reach California during the California gold rush starting in 1849. Another one hundred thousand well-intentioned souls headed to western Colorado near Pike's Peak in 1858 as part of the Pike's Peak gold rush.

Many of the people traveling west along the trail were ill prepared for the journey. They simply did not, or could not, bring enough food with them to sustain their journey, so they turned to hunting wild game, including birds, along the way.

The Homestead Act of 1862 allowed access to lands through the establishment of land claims that would be tended and farmed, which increased use of the westward routes into the plains. Although movies may depict the trails as long, lonely stretches of land with two tracks created by wheels of covered wagons, the trails were incredibly busy places. The Santa Fe Trail was busy enough to cause disruptions to the migration of bison, and railroads soon built tracks near the trails as well.

In 1916 Albert Leach published a memoir, *Early Day Stories*, in which he described the trip in 1852 that brought his family to the Nebraska Territory when he was a boy:

> Mr. Knapp went out with the rifle and shot the heads off of four or five wild pigeons. These were not the mourning or turtle dove, such as we have here now, but were the genuine passenger pigeon, now an extinct variety, but which were more abundant sixty years ago than blackbirds are today, and which were often seen in larger flocks than any flocks of blackbirds at the present.
>
> The little Indian (about twelve) found the place where I had cleaned the pigeons, and taking the entrails stripped them through his fingers so as to press out what was inside, and then boiled them with the gizzards, heads, and feet, upon the coals. These . . . were eaten with evident relish.

Alvin Osler moved with his family to Nebraska when he was thirteen years old. Two years later, his father died, and Alvin provided game as food for his family. He kept a log of his

PASSENGER PIGEON (*Columba Migratoria*)
Upper bird, female ; lower, male

37. Passenger pigeon (*upper* female, *lower* male). Engraving based on a painting by John J. Audubon, published 1840.

38. Henry M. Elsner hunting prairie-chickens near Grand Island, Nebraska, 1890. Photo from the collections of the Stuhr Museum of the Prairie Pioneer, used with permission.

hunting that included, in 1884, one hundred forty-eight greater prairie-chickens, sixty-five geese, thirty-four geese (most likely white-fronted geese; Osler referred to them as brant, a species of goose that only breeds and winters near coasts in North America), six ducks, six jack rabbits, and thirteen quail. Osler noted that prairie-chickens were hunted year-round, geese from March to April and October to November, ducks from March to April, and quail from January to October. Clearly, the birds near their farmstead were important as food items in the daily life of the family.

Market Hunting

Similar to the plains of Africa, the Great Plains became a safari grounds for hunters for recreational purposes, and some of these adventures included grand accommodations transported to a remote location. When Buffalo Bill hosted Grand Duke Alexis of Russia in southwest Nebraska during January of 1872, the *Sun* newspaper reported from North Platte, Nebraska:

> The permanent camp for the buffalo hunt is on Red Willow creek, about fifty miles southwest of this post. The camp consists of two hospital tents, ten wall tents and a tent for servants. Three of the wall tents are floored, and the Grand Duke's is carpeted. Box stoves and Sibley stoves are provided for the hospital and wall tents. The hospital tents are to be used as dining tents. An extensive culinary outfit was taken; also 10,000 rations each of flour, sugar, and coffee, and 1,000 pounds of tobacco for the Indians. Company K. second cavalry, Capt. Egan, is at the camp, and have everything in the best possible order. Company K, second cavalry, Lieut. Stover, acts as escort for the party. The whole is under the command of Gen. Palmer, of Omaha barracks. Lieut. Hayes is quartermaster of the expedition. Mr. Cody ("Buffalo Bill") met the party here. A relay of horses is at Medicine Creek, about half-way to the camp. The party expect to make the trip in eight hours. Buffaloes are in great numbers within ten miles of the camp. A few hours ago four hundred Indians were expected at the camp with their families, and others were coming in rapidly. It is expected that war parties of Spotted Tail, Whistler, War Bonnet, and Black Hat will be there, with their respective chiefs and bands. After the hunt there will be a grand Indian war dance, and provisions will be presented to the Indians if they behave themselves.

The visit of the Grand Duke was highly publicized and it brought others to the plains for hunting of bison and other species of game, including birds. Most other hunting parties were not as grand or as heavy on the logistics, and many consisted of enlisted military men who were stationed at posts throughout the plains, such as a party of soldiers from Fort Larned, Kansas, who took two hundred wild turkeys in a single day. We should remember that hunting regulations in the United States, in general, were near nonexistent, and the laws that were on the books were often not enforced. Law enforcement barely existed away from settlements in the western territories and states. The region was a playground for bank and train robbers and cattle thieves, so it is no wonder that wildlife laws were ignored by law enforcement teams busy chasing the Dalton Gang or the Black Hills Bandits.

In 1859 the Nebraska Territory closed the season between March 1 and July 15 for deer, elk, prairie-chicken, sharp-tailed grouse and woodcock, and in 1878 Iowa became the first state in the nation to impose a bag limit on a game species, which limited hunters to twenty-five greater prairie-chickens per day. But it would not be until 1913 that Pennsylvania became the first state to issue a hunting license. In the territories and newly founded states of the Great Plains region, imposing regulations on hunting was not the first priority of the new governments.

Although it may be easy for us to wish that hunting regulations had been stricter in the nineteenth century, it is impossible for us to imagine the bounty that seemed to greet the new residents of the plains, which teamed with animals to the extent that travelers excitedly wrote about their adventures. William Weston, in his *Guide to the Kansas Pacific Railway*, wrote in 1872:

> To the sportsman whose chief delight is in his breechloader and his pointers or setters the very finest sport may be had by getting off at any of the stations along the line from Kansas City to Salina. The whole of that country swarms with quail and prairie chickens. The abundance of quail may be

39. Depiction of hunters shooting prairie-chickens, titled "Our first shooting" from W. E. Webb, *Buffalo Land* (1872).

estimated by the fact that they are sold in the markets at $1 to $1½ per dozen and prairie chickens at $2½ per dozen. In the season a good shot can bag his 15 to 20 brace of quail per diem with ease.

Of course, Weston was writing to sell tickets on the railroad, so we might be hesitant to accept his flowery descriptions at face value. But journal after journal and book after book make it clear that bird numbers were high enough to afford hunters easy and fulfilling days in the field. Regarding a hunt in present-day Kansas, Lieutenant Colonel Richard Dodge wrote:

The most delightful hunting . . . I have ever had was in the country south-east of Fort Dodge on the small tributaries of the Cimarron River. I append the record of a hunt of twenty days in the section, in October 1872, in which one officer besides myself and three English gentlemen participated. Everything bagged was counted as one, and an idea of the spot can be formed from this list:

127 buffalo

2 deer (red) [modern name: elk]

11 antelope [pronghorn]

154 turkeys

5 geese

223 teal

45 mallard

49 shovel-bill [northern shoveler]

57 widgeon

38 butter-ducks [bufflehead]

3 shell-ducks [canvasback]

17 herons

143 meadowlarks, doves, robins, etc

6 cranes

187 quail

32 grouse

84 field-plover

33 yellow legs (snipe)

12 jack snipe [woodcock]

1 pigeon

9 hawks

3 owls

2 badgers

7 racoons [*sic*]

11 rattlesnakes

1 blue bird for his sweetheart's hat

Total head bagged: 1,262

In 1876 the *Ellsworth, Kansas, Reporter* noted that three men bagged sixty-four prairie-chickens on a Saturday. Three years later, the same paper reported that seven men had returned to this Kansas town from a hunt at a salt marsh along the Arkansas River with one hundred twenty-one geese, sixty ducks, twenty

Big Bird

THE first time he ever fired his dad's shotgun Willard Boesiger of Gage county brought down big game — an American eagle 7 feet from wing tip to wing tip and 3 feet from head to tip of tail. The big bird was in a tree in the Boesigers' front yard. It was only stunned by the shot and, before he finally killed it, Willard kept the live eagle in a cage for several weeks.

The Nebraska Farmer, January 16, 1937

40. A juvenile bald eagle, with mottled dark and white wings, shot by a youth. *Nebraska Farmer* magazine, January 16, 1937, used with permission.

jack snipes (now called woodcock), and five cranes. The reporter noted that the gentlemen "had a good time."

Other normal, but wide-eyed citizens reported their adventures to the local newspaper in efforts that might be interpreted as making a survey of what existed in the region. At the same time that bears and mountain lions were being shot and removed from the landscape to reduce threat to livestock and people, large owls and bald eagles with eight-foot wingspans were also killed, apparently for curiosity's sake (figure 40). "White cranes," potentially whooping cranes but more likely egrets, were taken by hunters as well, and the *Saline County Journal*, in 1873, reported that H. C. Knox had killed a large swan: "He brought it to Major Probert's drug store, where it was upon exhibition for several hours and attracted considerable attention. Its beautiful plumage elicited many words of admiration from a number who had, for the first time, seen a swan."

Killing birds for the sake of curiosity lasted into the next century, well beyond the passage of the Migratory Bird Treaty Act in 1918, which makes illegal the taking of all birds native to the United States as well as their nests and eggs. Raptors were commonly killed to protect livestock and pets, but the Bald and Golden Eagle Protection Act of 1940 added further federal penalties for killing or disturbing bald and golden eagles.

Early settlers on the plains used game largely for sustenance, but with the railroads came additional pressure from outside the plains. Albert Leach, the Nebraska immigrant author, describes the new dynamic as he remembered it: "Game was seldom, if ever, hunted for the market in those days, but was killed only to supply home demands. The prairie chicken hunters had not reached Antelope County in those days. These hunters, and the rats, came at the same time. They both came with the railroad, but not before."

As Leach outlined, market hunters used the railroads to establish what we would call, in modern terms, a farm-to-table distribution network that used the Great Plains as a resource for game animals that would arrive in time to be served in Chicago or New York City at private homes or fine restaurants. A census in 1886 revealed that only 540 bison remained in the entire United States, and most of these had retreated into harder-to-access areas of the Rocky Mountains, such as the valleys of Yellowstone. However, birds remained abundant on the plains for market hunters.

Detective work by James Ducey has chronicled the markets for passenger pigeons and other game animals that were available to market hunters. During April to June of 1867, nearly one hundred thousand passenger pigeons were sold in one game market in Chicago, Illinois, and more than two hundred meat markets existed in 1867 in Chicago. If we factor in other cities and destinations for game, it becomes clear that large numbers of animals were being shipped out of the plains. The pattern of trade foreshadows today's grain markets and similar uses of plains states to feed the country and the world.

But the markets were not always farther east. During the building of railroads the workers needed food, and local hunters sold ducks, geese, grouse, and snipe (in addition to buffalo, elk, and pronghorn) to railroads for prices ranging from fifty cents per pair for prairie-chickens to $1.50 each for geese. Demand for food from the plains meant that ducks, geese, and prairie-chickens could be sold at local city markets in Nebraska in the 1880s for lofty prices of two to four dollars per dozen, which is well over fifty to one hundred dollars today, accounting for inflation. The demand and initial lack of law enforcement encouraged hunters and marketers to ignore any laws that existed. A market report in February 1887 included this statement: "Prairie chickens, quail, and venison are out of season and it is contrary to the law for dealers to handle them. The law has never been very strictly enforced, and a good many dealers handle them after they are out of season."

The market for buffalo hides is better known than markets for birds, because we have been swamped with images of skinned bison dotting the prairie landscape and piles of skulls and bones collected to use for fertilizer. The hunting of birds was also prevalent on the plains, but the practice left no carcasses on the landscape and few traces of other evidence. Perhaps we suffer the impression that most market hunters focused on bison, or perhaps we surmise that those commercial hunters who killed birds did so when they could not find bison. We may also visualize these hunters toiling on the plains alone, bringing their bags of birds to a train terminal where they were packaged and sent eastward in a smallish box. Nothing, it turns out, could be further from the truth. Market hunting for birds was a well-oiled machine with collection points, salaried shooters, and support staff. Consider this cautionary description from northeastern Nebraska from Samuel Griswold, a sports writer for the *Omaha Bee* newspaper, who was beginning to fear the results of market hunting on wildlife and society:

> Last fall I indulged in a three weeks' outing in the northwestern part of the State, and at no less than five different points on the B. & M. road did I visit the rendezvous of Eastern market-hunters, who have built permanent shipping establishments, with refrigerative annexes and shipping departments, and carry on their unlawful business regularly all the year round openly and defiantly. These shippers not only employ all the farmers' boys they can roundabout the country, but they bring in expert shots from the East, whom they pay a regular salary for their work in the field. Now is not this a sad commentary upon the laws of a great and progressive State like Nebraska; isn't it an unqualified disgrace and an outrage, and does it not call for a loud protest from every true sportsman in the State, and a vigorous remonstrance from all our lovers of nature? I think so.

Lack of dependable refrigeration was the single wrench in the works of the distribution network system of game birds from the plains. Each bird had an expiration date enforced by Mother Nature, and time was of the essence if the product was to reach its destination in condition to be sold. We can imagine the odors involved at markets for wild game in those days. The effects

41. Wild birds for sale at the F. M. Smith and Co. Game market in Chicago, Illinois, between 1895 and 1910. Photo originally published by Detroit Publishing Company, from the collections of the Library of Congress L C-D 4–43098.

of this problem are evident in a strong-smelling report from a market in Chicago in September 1878: "The warm weather for the past few days has been unfavorable, and a considerable portion of the receipts are coming in in bad order, and quite a number of birds have been confiscated by the health officers."

Spoiled meat left a bad taste in the mouths of members of the dining public, we can assume, and likewise society eventually began to understand how commercial hunting was dismantling wildlife populations. Enforcement of game laws was lacking on the Great Plains during the latter part of the nineteenth century, but the wholesale decline of the buffalo had ruffled conservation feathers to the east. Newspaper editors had started

to apply pressure, and gun clubs, sporting clubs, and conservation organizations such as the League of American Sportsmen,
the American Ornithologist's Union, the Camp Fire Club, the
New York Zoological Society, the Audubon Society, and the
American Bison Society formed in part to support the cause
of conservation in the west. These new lobbyists pushed for
enforcement of existing laws and new laws that would protect
game species, including birds. An editorial from February 1874
in the *Journal* of Lincoln, Nebraska, was an early voice for
conservation:

> There is no law for the protection of the buffalo. The conse-
> quence is that these animals are being slaughtered at such a
> wholesale rate as will insure their total destruction within a
> very few years. The extent to which this slaughter is carried on
> is incredible. In the western portion of this state their carcasses
> are so thickly strewn that a gentleman informs us he could
> stand at any point and count five hundred carcasses. . . . That
> a terrible warfare is being waged against these poor brutes is
> certain from the fact that one firm on the U.P. railroad has
> been shipping their hides at a rate of 500 a day. . . . There
> are hunters who follow the business of killing these animals
> merely for their hides, sometimes not removing any portion
> of the meat but leaving it to rot on the plains. . . . It would
> be a burning shame if the buffalo should be wiped from the
> face of the earth. Let us have a law to protect the buffalo.

A report from a market in Chicago, in 1875, suggested that the
pressure was starting to affect the sale of game taken elsewhere
at eastern markets: "The Gun Clubs are making quite an effort
to enforce the law. Still, dealers insist that it does not imply on
through stuff [hunted birds moved from one place to another]
or on birds killed in other States, and a test case will probably
be had to settle the matter. The Produce Exchange, through a

committee, will petition the Legislature for a change from the present law on Game."

Change happens slowly, and it was 1900 before the U.S. Congress passed the Lacey Game and Wild Birds Preservation and Disposition Act, which made it a federal crime to transport game across state borders if it had been taken illegally in another state. At the same time, the young states of the Great Plains were maturing. The state wildlife agencies that we know today were created during this period: Montana in 1885, Colorado in 1897, Nebraska in 1901, Kansas in 1905, Texas in 1907, Oklahoma and North Dakota in 1909, New Mexico in 1912, and South Dakota in 1918. Some states paid early game wardens, while others used a cadre of volunteer wardens who reported illegal acts involving fish and wildlife to local police. In some cases, the volunteers earned half of the fines that were leveled because of the warden's actions. The increased level of law enforcement at the state level and the passage of the Lacey Act spelled the end of the game markets in Chicago, New York City, and elsewhere. Unregulated market hunting was over.

Redesigning Avian Communities

The early twentieth century was a dynamic time with regard to birds in the Great Plains. The last documented, wild passenger pigeon had been shot in 1901. With protection, other game-bird numbers were recovering. However, habitats were changing as agriculture was established, and several species of birds were introduced to the Great Plains from Europe and Asia. Of course, the world would soon be dealing with increasing global challenges that led to World War I, the Great Depression, and World War II in the space of two generations. Mechanization was leading to modifications in lifestyles—indeed, it was a period defined by massive changes. It would have been an incredibly confusing time to be alive, I think.

In that context, consider one reflection on the trajectories of populations of birds during this period written in 1907 by William Stolley, an immigrant from Germany to Nebraska in the 1850s. Stolley embodies a dual perspective with regard to conservation. He documents and laments the loss of species of wildlife from his region, while in other writings he describes how he poisoned ten wolves that had tried to steal his food soon after he immigrated to the plains. With modern-day hindsight, we can find similar irony in the fact that Stolley regretted the changes that humans had wrought upon the bird species of the plains, yet he was proud to have helped introduce from Europe what we now call the house sparrow:

Especially in the case of wild fowl has so-called "civilized society," which crowded out the Indians, demonstrated that it must have descended from vandals. They kill, destroy, and shoot at them until there is nothing left to shoot.

All rivers and creeks were alive with beaver, otter, mink, muskrats and raccoons, along with various kinds of geese, ducks, pelicans, swans, and other water birds. These birds of passage appeared by the thousands every spring and fall. Cranes, gray and white, and several species of wood cocks were seen in large flocks. All this had changed entirely in the fifty years that have passed since the founding of our settlement. The above-mentioned birds and animals whose great multitudes gave the land its peculiar character and appeal in those early days have decreased in numbers to almost the vanishing point.

On the other hand, it must be affirmed that the world of song and other small birds has increased enormously, probably due to the plantings of woods and shrubs which offer them a better opportunity for building nests.

Prairie chickens and quail also are more numerous than they were in the early years. They multiplied very rapidly, as wolves and foxes were greatly decimated in a few years by poisoning. Later, when the railroad reached us, the flocks of prairie chickens and quail were cleaned up in a few years so that game laws were necessary to prevent their complete extermination. Now, these birds, so useful to the farmer, are again increasing rapidly in numbers.

That is a question which arises involuntarily in my mind. If things go on in as senseless a manner as in the past, then of the wild fowl, probably only the European sparrow will remain. I imported the birds from New York early in May 1876, in the hope of using them to combat migratory grasshoppers. For 24 years since I set free five pair of these sparrows on our farm, they have proven themselves worthy representatives of their tribe, and seem to be ever mindful of the command of their Creator, "be fruitful and multiply."

When fifty more years have passed into oblivion and all wildfowl can only be seen as mounted specimens in museums, I hope that the hotels and restaurants in Grand Island will still serve delicious sparrow pie at a reasonable price.

What about these new introductions to the plains? With such a diverse bird community, why did people feel the need to introduce more birds around cities and farmsteads?

One of the first documented introductions of birds, although caged, to the Great Plains can be found in the photos of Solomon Butcher, a photographer in north-central Nebraska during the latter part of the nineteenth century. Butcher did not excel at farming, so he opened a photography business in Custer County, Nebraska. He went from farm to farm, taking farmstead portraits of families, with promises to return in a few weeks with the finished photograph. Most farmers in Custer County lived in sod houses, and Butcher typically arranged the photos with the family situated in front of their house to

42. John Curry and his wife in front of their sod house near West Union, Nebraska. This Solomon Butcher photo has often been referred to as "Nebraska Gothic" and may have influenced Grant Wood's *American Gothic* painting. A birdcage hangs with a canary inside the open doorway. Items of interest have been arranged behind the couple and their dog. The original glass plate used to make the photograph has been damaged. From the collections of the Nebraska State Historical Society and the Library of Congress, used with permission.

show off their handiwork. The family often selected items to include in the photo, such as their piano or special chairs or a pile of elk antlers. Perhaps they were sending a message to their friends or relatives that might receive a copy of the photograph that all was well on the plains? Regardless, Butcher's work has become a well-studied archive that describes life in the 1880s on the plains, and many of the photos show canaries in cages hanging from the side of the sod house or sitting on furniture, posed for the camera (figure 42).

Why canaries? In the 1800s canaries were popular in cities in the eastern U.S., and a handful of traders made a fortune shipping canaries to be purchased in San Francisco during the California gold rush. My guess is that canaries were a signal of civilization to these hearty, yet fragile families living in a sod house on the plains with fires and thunderstorms and plagues of locusts and droughts posing constant danger to their existence. If you can imagine going to sleep with rodents scurrying beneath your bed and snakes falling from the ceiling after a hard day in the rain or scorching sun, perhaps a sweetly singing, yellow bird was more of a psychiatric tool than a pet?

Ring-necked pheasants are a popular game bird in the Great Plains. The fact that pheasants are the official bird of South Dakota is evidence of the birds' importance to the economics of rural towns throughout the plains where hunters descend in the fall. However, pheasants are not a native species of the United States. China is the origin of ring-necked pheasants, and the species has all of the characteristics needed to encourage humans to distribute it throughout the world. It is a handsome bird as the males have iridescent purple feathers on the head. Pheasants are tasty to eat, a good size as a hunter's quarry, fairly easy to rear in captivity, and adaptable to a variety of climates and habitats. England has stocked pheasants for hunting for over a thousand years, and ring-necked pheasants have been introduced throughout Europe, northern Africa, Australia, Chile, and many Pacific islands. In the late 1700s and 1800s, several attempts were made to introduce pheasants to North America, and the first successful attempt was in Oregon in the 1880s, with birds from Shanghai.

South Dakota's first introduction of pheasants occurred in 1909, and we have never looked back. State wildlife agencies obtained birds in lots of twenty to three hundred at a time and released them in local environments that were favorable—landscapes with many acres covered by small-grain crops (wheat, barley, oats, and sorghum), grasslands, and fields with winter cover and food. In 1919 the first pheasant season was opened in South Dakota, and Nebraska had its first season in 1927. Sportsmen were asked to help propagate the species, and 230 game farms received permits to raise pheasants in Nebraska.

Not everyone was happy to see pheasants introduced. "There is little doubt but the birds are injurious to farm crops in certain regions," wrote Glenn Buck for the *Nebraska Farmer* in September 1928. Buck reported that his publication had received so many letters complaining about pheasants that "it would be impossible to publish all of them."

An attempt in 1928 by the U.S. Department of Agriculture to document wild birds introduced or transplanted in North America begins: "The early history of the introduction of foreign birds into this country is clothed in darkness." As was the case for pheasants, private individuals tried to release many alien bird species with the best of intentions but without any of the current controls and regulation enforced by our customs officials. The USDA report continues:

> There are at least two schools of thought on the subject of introducing and transplanting birds, and these are widely at variance. One of these, the conservative, represented by such eminent naturalists as Joseph Grinnell of California and many others, believes in preserving at all costs the present or rather the original status of native birds and harmless mammals, and points out the great dangers incurred in the importation of new species in other parts of the world, and especially the danger of spreading new diseases. The other school would bring in anything from a button quail to an ostrich without any regard to the general suitability of the species. Most sportsmen and naturalists do not agree fully

with either of these views, although the writer sympathizes strongly with the first. It is, of course, known that it is impossible to maintain our bird fauna at anything like its original balance, whether new varieties are introduced or not, because of man's operations over the face of nature.

In the early twentieth century, many referred to avian introductions as innovative experiments. The author of the 1928 USDA publication may have been cautious about general introductions, but in regard to the Formosan teal from China, a brilliantly colored waterfowl with gold and green patches on its head, a comment was inserted: "This would be an interesting species to try out on a large scale."

Large-scale experiments were indeed happening and would continue to happen throughout North America. The common inhabitant of urban areas, the rock pigeon was introduced from Europe in the 1600s in Nova Scotia, Virginia, and Massachusetts, and it is now found throughout the United States. The house sparrow also came from Europe in a series of initial introductions in New York City; Portland, Maine; Peace Dale, Rhode Island; and Boston, Massachusetts, between 1851 and 1869. Several other introductions occurred and translocations brought birds from the east to the Great Plains. Accounts at the time suggested that towns near railroads were more likely to have house sparrows.

If you have been offended by the European starling, you owe your disgust to a unique club in New York City that established the goal of introducing all of the birds mentioned in Shakespeare's plays to North America. Seriously. About one hundred pairs of starlings were released in 1890 and 1891 in Central Park in New York City, and all because of this single, solitary line in *Henry IV*, uttered by Hotspur: "Nay, I will; that's flat: He said he would not ransom Mortimer; forbad my tongue to speak of Mortimer; but I will find him when he lies asleep, and in his ear I'll holla 'Mortimer!' Nay, I'll have a starling shall be taught to speak nothing but 'Mortimer,' and give it him to keep his anger still in motion."

The gray partridge, often referred to as the Hungarian partridge, was introduced in a lot of forty thousand birds in 1908 and 1909 from Europe as a game bird. It is found throughout the northern plains states, and sportsmen were anxious to introduce partridge because of how the English talked about the species: "The advantage of turning out Hungarian birds cannot be overestimated. They are suitable from every point of view—stronger and hardier than our native birds and therefore more capable of rearing large coveys." Early reports from Kansas, where the partridges are not found today, indicate that after stocking them in the winter of 1909, the birds "have made no showing whatever." Just to the north, in Nebraska, partridges initially took to the landscape, with wardens reporting that "the birds were distributed throughout the State and appear to have done well."

The house finch's introduction to the Great Plains is full of geographic twists and turns. Before 1940 the house finch was found originally in the western United States and Mexico, reaching as far east as southeastern Wyoming, western Nebraska, western Kansas, western Oklahoma, and central Texas. However, an illegal attempt to sell caged house finches under the cage trade name "Hollywood finches" in New York City resulted in release of the species when the sellers could not find homes for the birds. Over the next few decades, house finches spread westward, making it to Chicago in the 1970s and Nebraska and Kansas in the 1980s. Across the plains, sightings of house finches and nesting records suggest that the original western and introduced eastern populations have merged into a single population.

Two other nonnative birds, the Eurasian collared dove and the cattle egret, have moved into the Great Plains after securing footholds in Caribbean islands before moving ashore. They were not purposefully released on the continent, however. Worldwide, the movement of nonnative fish, mammals, birds, insects, reptiles, and amphibians into new regions is becoming more of the norm than an unusual occurrence. While biologists struggle to control and confine zebra mussels or species of Asian carp in Great Plains lakes and rivers, other biologists are purposefully managing habitat to increase numbers of ring-necked pheasants. All are introduced species, but we label zebra mussels and Asian carp as invasive, capable of exponential increases in numbers and with high potential to cause negative ecosystem impacts. The distinction is important, as biologists prioritize efforts to work with nonnative species in an ever-changing world.

Climate Change

Ask any gardener or farmer in the Great Plains, and they will tell you—the climate has changed in measurable ways during their lives. Plant Hardiness Zones were changed recently—affecting where garden centers would suggest certain plants to be used, and projections are that in the next thirty years, these zones will shift more dramatically. Farmers are adapting by planting corn and soybean strains with longer growing seasons, and in some places they are, for the first time, able to plant two short-season crops in the same year. It stands to reason that birds are responding to climate change as well.

The warming trend in climate can be seen in the documented earliest arrivals of pelicans at a wildlife refuge in North Dakota across forty-four years of observation. On average, by 2008, the birds were steadily arriving ten days earlier than they did in 1965 (figure 43). Biologists who study cliff swallows on the Great Plains report similar trends—mud nests are now patched and

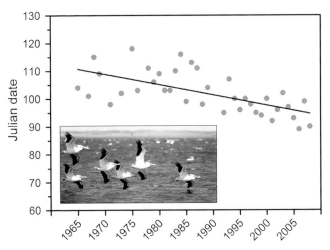

43. The date that American white pelicans first arrived each year at a breeding colony in Chase Lake National Wildlife Refuge in Stutsman County, North Dakota, during a forty-four-year period (1965–2008). Julian dates are days after January 1 each year; day 60 is March 1, day 100 is April 10, and day 120 is April 30. Data source: M. A. Sovada et al., "Influence of Climate Change on Productivity of American White Pelicans, *Pelecanus erythrorhynchos*," PLOS ONE 9, no. 1 (2014): e:83430. Photo by Rick Bohn, USFWS.

built nine days earlier, on average, than in 1983. Migratory birds are able to arrive earlier and stay later because of the warmer climate. If you stayed awake through chapter 2, on the geologic history of the Great Plains, you may also remember that during the last Ice Age, the central plains were home to birds that now live in Alaska. Birds have wings, and they can shift—right? No big deal. Longer summers means more beach time for us, as well.

Yes, birds can shift their migration dates; but in many cases, birds are not shifting fast enough. Biologists report that the bloom of insects that occurs in the spring and rewards our north-bound feathered friends are also shifting in time. Many species of birds are finding that the insects they need have hatched and died by the time the birds arrive at migratory stopovers or breeding grounds. The migration timing of birds and their food source is now mismatched, resulting in food shortages for the birds.

Shifting migration dates are not the only story when we consider climate change and its potential impact on birds, because a changing climate brings changes in seasonal weather as well. My father, a farmer in Iowa, recently installed prairie strips in his fields to control rainwater during large rains. He has seen stronger storms and more large rain events recently, and the protection measures for soil that he had in place were no longer holding. He needed a new tool to save his soil. In similar fashion, birds are experiencing more dramatic weather events. When chicks first leave the nest, the systems used to regulate their body temperature are still coming online, you might say. And their tiny bodies have very little mass in their core to buffer against cold temperatures. A rainstorm and cold temperatures in the spring can kill baby birds, and large rain events that continue for several hours or over a series of days produce unrelenting attacks on young chicks. Climate change has the potential to affect productivity of birds, which is especially concerning for birds like Attwater's prairie-chicken, whooping cranes, or piping plovers—species in which every hatchling holds the future of the species on its shoulders.

Some birds will benefit from climate change as they are able to expand their range (figure 44). We generally predict birds may shift north as warming occurs, but what if a species reaches the northern edge of the continent? Biologists are predicting that breeding grounds for birds in northern Canada, on the edge of the Arctic, will warm to the extent that they are no longer useful for these species. Geese and shorebirds are likely to be affected the most.

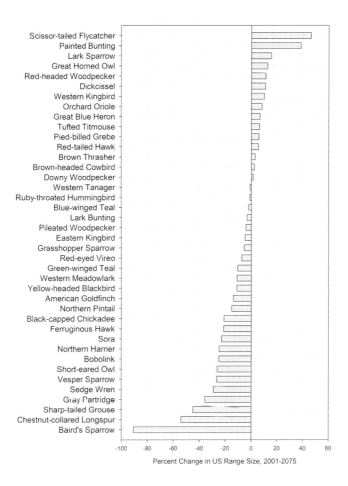

44. Predicted changes for select Great Plains birds for the size of species' range in the United States as a function of climate change and changing land cover and land use. Public data for average climate scenarios from T. Sohl, USGS.

Birds are constantly battling parasites, and warmer climates will most likely result in longer periods during which parasites such as blood-sucking mites in nests and ticks are able to build their populations to higher levels than at present. Yuck, I know. The result would be lower production of young and lower survival of adults that could lead to slow population declines.

Oceans are expected to suffer direct effects of climate change because of melting ice caps at the poles, and sea level is already changing along our coasts. Ocean currents are affected by water temperature, and oceans are warming each year. Ocean temperature also affects formation and strength of hurricanes. Although all of those factors seem far removed from the Great Plains, many of our migratory birds spend the better part of their year on beaches and in coastal wetlands. Hurricanes pose a risk to endangered whooping cranes and piping plovers that winter along coasts during hurricane season. Coastal beaches, used by shorebirds during the winter, are now a potential pinch-point for birds, because human-built landscapes define a back edge to most coastal beaches. Current conservation efforts attempt to help birds such as piping plovers survive the winter on developed beaches, but climate change seems destined to cause greater erosion to the seaward edge of coastal beaches during stronger storms, and the beach may be subsumed by rising sea levels. Only two centuries ago, beach erosion or sea-level change resulted in natural movements of beaches back onto previous high ground, and oceans have rebuilt shorelines for eons. However, buildings and highways now occupy the space behind most beaches. There is often no open land for beach expansion, leaving little room for birds attempting to adapt to a changing environment. Even in the plains, we cannot forget about oceans as we talk about climate change and our birds.

Any bird will tell you that two factors determine where they and their fellow sparrows or ducks or hawks are located on the global map: the land cover or habitat that is available at a given spot on the earth and the climate—chiefly temperature and precipitation (figure 45). We can gaze at the range maps available in identification books for birds and pick out forest birds, wetland birds, and grassland birds. We can also find birds that seem to enjoy breeding in cooler, wetter regions and birds that are found in hotter and drier conditions. The best predictions that are available for farmers and gardeners suggest that warming temperatures will bring with them changes in precipitation, which will fundamentally change the land cover and land use across the globe. Baird's sparrow, for example, is a Great Plains endemic with a small range in the northern plains, and the sparrow has specific moisture requirements and is intolerant to fluctuations in temperature. Climate change will most likely remove it from the United States as it shifts to acceptable conditions that are predicted eventually to occur only in Canada. In similar fashion, biologists predict that the range of ferruginous hawks will shrink in the southern portion of their range due to warming and drying in that region, while losses in the hawks' range in the Dakotas will occur with predicted losses of grassland due to changing land use under new climate conditions (Figure 45). It is no wonder that birds spend an inordinate amount of time talking about the future of our planet as they hop from bush to bush, foraging for insects.

The dynamics of landscape composition as climate changes is a concern to conservation groups in the Great Plains, such as Ducks Unlimited, World Wildlife Fund, The Nature Conservancy, the U.S. Fish and Wildlife Service, and the Audubon Society. For example, warmer climates and changes in precipitation are expected to change wetland landscapes: warmer temperatures cause evaporation, and droughts will occur at higher frequency. Both dynamics may result in over half of the wetlands in the Great Plains drying beyond usefulness to

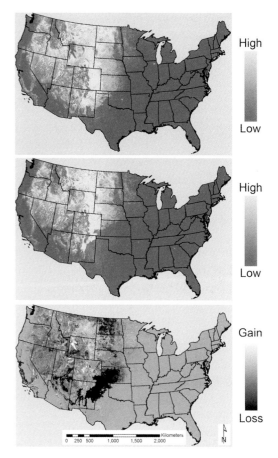

45. Ferruginous hawk distribution in 2001 (*top*), predicted distribution in 2100 (*middle*), and areas of change (*bottom*). Predicted distribution is modeled as a combination of environmental climate effects and land use effects, driven by climate change as predicted by the Intergovernmental Panel on Climate Change A2 scenario. Due to a hotter and drier climate by 2100, ferruginous hawks will lose range along the southeastern edge of their current distribution, while a loss of grassland habitat results in range loss in the Dakotas. Analysis by T. Sohl, USGS, used with permission.

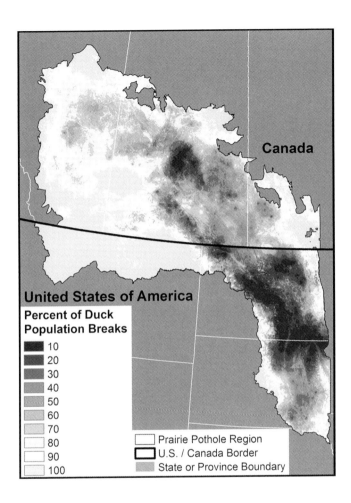

46. Average relative abundance of five species of dabbling ducks (blue-winged teal, gadwall, mallard, northern pintail, and northern shoveler) across the U.S. and Canadian Prairie Pothole Region during 2002–10. *Dark colors* represent the core breeding areas. Image by K. Doherty and colleagues.

breeding birds—a huge impact on the North American "duck factory" of the northern plains (figure 46) that depends on the potholes in the prairie. Grasslands will also be affected by climate change, as species of plants will respond differently to higher amounts of carbon dioxide in the air and warmer temperatures. The effects of climate change on land cover are difficult to predict, but changes in the face of the Great Plains may have the largest effect on birds of any possible factor.

People are also affected by climate change, and our ability to carry out conservation strategies to manage birds will also change as our climate warms. It should be clear by this point that we must make careful decisions to manage the remaining habitat patches in the Great Plains. Water levels in wetlands of wildlife refuges require pumping of groundwater into impoundments to maintain water levels during droughts. Grassland fragments require prescribed burning to reduce encroachment of trees. We now actively work to maintain and restore bird populations, and each of our public land areas in the Great Plains is an island in a sea of agriculture. Less than 2 percent of the Great Plains is managed as national park, national forest, national wildlife refuge, or state wildlife areas, but they are managed intensively to produce habitat to benefit specific species of birds and other wildlife. As climate change affects the ranges of birds, some species will be forced off the ranch, so to speak—the temperature or rainfall level at a management area may no longer be suitable for that species. Birds may have to shift and find another managed area to the north for breeding or for a migratory stopover site. Wildlife managers will have to develop flexible and creative plans to deal with shifting bird communities on their reserves, which are often steeped in tradition. Is it fair to say that state and federal governments are not known for the speed of their reactions when change is needed? We will have to do better in the future, and visitors and bird watchers will have to accept that the species they found five years ago during a holiday birding trip may no longer be present in the same location.

Birds of the Great Plains have endured a variety of pressures and constraints caused by human use of landscapes in the past, and climate change will have broad impacts on birds in future.

CHAPTER FOUR

The Hope

Conservation Strategies

Early Conservation of Birds

Samuel Clemens, better known to his readers as Mark Twain, traveled across the Great Plains in the midst of the westward movement of immigrants from Europe and the eastern United States. Clemens lived during the transition period for wildlife on the plains, when bison had been severely reduced, but other species could still enthrall travelers with their omnipresence. Clemens wrote of the vastness of nature and the wonders of biodiversity in a letter to his future wife, Olivia Langdon, in January of 1870:

> I do not see how astronomers can help feeling exquisitely insignificant, for every new page of the Book of the Heavens they open reveals to them more and more that the world we are so proud of is to the universe of careening globes as is one mosquito to the winged and hoofed flocks and herds that darken the air and populate the plains and forests of all the earth. If you killed the mosquito would it be missed? Verily, What is Man, that he should be considered of God?

It is still easy for a visitor to the Great Plains to gain insight into the concept of our human place in the world—a sense of smallness in the midst of the vast plains. But by the turn of the twentieth century, there had been a thinning of the winged flocks that darkened the air on the plains as Clemens had viewed them.

Early conservation efforts in North America attempted to preserve land to support wildlife. The Boone and Crockett Club had formed in 1887 to protect big-game animals, especially in the American West, and the club worked with their most famous member, Theodore Roosevelt, to plan a series of wildlife refuges across the United States. The first of the national wildlife refuges was designated in coastal Florida in 1903 to protect waterbirds from hunters who sold feathers for ladies' hats.

The Wichita Mountains Forest and Game Reserve, later to become the Wichita Mountains Wildlife Refuge, was one of the first public areas to be designated in the Great Plains in 1905. The federal government continued to support conservation of birds through the passage of the Weeks-McLean Act in 1913, which recognized that waterfowl are more effectively managed across state boundaries rather than state by state, as other wildlife are managed by state wildlife agencies. From this point forward, waterfowl harvest regulations were set by the federal government.

A brilliant moment for conservation occurred in 1934 with the sale of the first Duck Stamp (figure 47). The stamp and those that followed it each year were works of art. Nonhunting collectors still purchase them, and artists compete to have their work chosen for each year's unique design. Since 1934, hunters have been required to place a Duck Stamp on their hunting license as a second requirement and as a part of the fee for legal waterfowl hunting. Today, Ducks Stamps also provide free entry if a national wildlife refuge charges an entry fee. The stamps now generate more than $25 million per year, and the funds are used to purchase or manage habitat for waterfowl. Almost six million acres in the United States have been acquired for

47. The first Duck Stamp depicting a pair of mallards, issued in 1934–35 by the U. S. Department of Agriculture migratory bird office and drawn by Jay N. "Ding" Darling, chief of the U.S. Biological Survey. Image provided by U.S. Fish and Wildlife Service.

public use with duck stamp funds, which includes all or part of three hundred national wildlife refuges. As you visit any of the wildlife refuges listed in chapter 5 of this book, think about all of the individual sales of Duck Stamps to eager hunters and conservation enthusiasts that support a system of public lands that has no equal in the world.

The innovative step taken with the sale of the Duck Stamp was to turn hunters from being the problem to solving the problem. After the period of unregulated market hunting in the United States, hunting was quite rightly seen as a major factor in the decline of wildlife in the Great Plains and beyond. Regulations were slow to take effect—it was 1913 before Pennsylvania became the first state to issue hunting licenses in an attempt to monitor and limit hunting. Duck Stamps were a tool to bring hunters into line and support the resource that they used. The negative, national opinion toward hunters can be symbolized by this 1933 editorial in *Nature Magazine* published by the American Nature Association:

> This hunter, having paid his license fee and quipped himself, is privileged, if he can find them, to kill each hunting day for about two months fifteen ducks, four geese, twenty-five rails and gallinules, twenty-five coots, twenty Wilson's snipe, four woodcock, and eighteen mourning doves among the migratory species . . . ostensibly he is forbidden to bait doves with grain or water, but he invents ways to defeat the spirit of the law, and if his hand is not stayed we shall see the mourning dove follow the passenger pigeon. He may not sell game, but he can buy the privilege of killing it by methods totally devoid of sportsmanship. He may not shoot ducks from an airplane, but he can hire the same airplane to drive them from a sanctuary to his blind. Of course, this is not hunting, because the waterfowl killer merely conceals himself and shoots the birds that are lured or driven to his gun. . . .
>
> America's game birds are fast vanishing. When will the true sportsmen of America—for there are some—begin serious efforts to purge their ranks of the slaughterers? They must begin soon, if they wish to save the game.

The Dust Bowl and Great Depression descended on the Great Plains during the 1930s. At the same time that Duck Stamps were issued for the first time, this period of major drought was about to set a political climate that would forever change conservation of soil, water, and wildlife in the United States. Farms were going under financially as multiple seasons of failed crops hit farmers directly in the pocketbook. Seeking to keep farmers on the farm, the federal government passed the 1933 Agriculture Adjustment Act, which featured direct payments to farmers who reduced output of certain commodities for

48. Cartoon by Jay N. "Ding" Darling, September 17, 1930. Courtesy of the Jay N. "Ding" Darling Wildlife Society and with permission of the University of Iowa Libraries, Special Collections Department.

price relief. However, the Supreme Court ruled that the new law was not constitutional—public money, the Court asserted, could not be used to support specific individuals.

Farmers still were in desperate need of cash as the Depression deepened. The key to a political solution was to find a way to pay farmers that would be seen as a public good, to justify the payments. The clever response was the Soil Conservation Act of 1935, which brought payments to farmers who used conservation practices. Conservation of soil and water was certainly seen to be in the public interest, especially when newspapers carried images of soil blowing across the plains. Farmers, at least the ones who remained on the farm, got relief and a precedent for the federal government to support conservation in the context of agricultural policy was set.

The Soil Conservation Act has been modified many times over the years, and we know it today as the farm bill. Farmers who qualify for conservation programs are paid to grow grass or trees rather than crops, which supports removal of nitrates from our streams among other benefits. In 1986 wildlife benefits were added to federal conservation programs, which have allowed farmers to plan conservation practices that benefit wildlife directly. One of the prime programs in the farm bill is the Conservation Reserve Program, which provides for ten-year contracts between farmers and the federal government. Approximately 24 million acres, or 37,500 square miles (the size of half of South Dakota, if we were to dump all conservation acres into one lump) of farmland are enrolled in the Conservation Reserve Program nationwide, and many of those acres are in states of the Great Plains. Grassland birds, including ducks in the Prairie Pothole region, have benefited greatly from more grass on the landscape. It is amazing to think that we have these programs today, largely because of a legal maneuver that used conservation to save farmers during the Great Depression.

Funding Modern Wildlife Management

Another critical piece in the conservation puzzle was added in 1937, the Pittman-Robertson Federal Aid in Wildlife Restoration Act. Prior to 1937, state wildlife agencies operated on lean budgets with many volunteer efforts. Certainly, little money existed to do any meaningful habitat management on state lands. The supporters of the Wildlife Restoration Act worked with the gun and ammunition manufacturers on a special deal. Given the drastic reductions in numbers of game animals, there was soon to be no game for hunters to hunt and, thus, no hunters. If there were no hunters, who would buy guns and ammunition? Following the same logic used in passage of Duck Stamp legislation, the Pittman-Robertson Act placed a tax of 11 percent on guns and ammunition sold in the United States. The act is still in place today, and the funds are collected by the U.S. Fish and Wildlife Service and distributed back to the states in the form of grants to pay for wildlife restoration projects, research, and education. When you visit a state wildlife area, or if you read about a research project conducted on game animals by your state's university, odds are that the support funds come from Pittman-Robertson funds.

What does the future hold for conservation? Certainly, there are many challenges for birds in the Great Plains. But conservation organizations continue to develop innovative solutions to protect, manage, and support wildlife on our lands. Nongame birds and endangered species currently have less funding for conservation than do game birds. State agencies and other groups have struggled for years to pull together funds to work on our songbirds and shorebirds and raptors—birds that do not typically benefit directly from Duck Stamps or Pittman-Robertson Act funding. Unfortunately, the act of listing a species as threatened or endangered does not guarantee that any money will be available to fund its recovery plan. The U.S. Congress has to approve funding for recovery of wildlife species, and wildlife competes with education, defense, social welfare and all other priorities of our nation.

In December of 2017, U.S. legislators introduced a new bill, the Recovering America's Wildlife Act, which would support conservation of species at risk by providing funds to state wildlife agencies. The funds are intended to keep species from becoming threatened and endangered—thus allowing more local and state control rather than federal oversight with the Endangered Species Act. The bill was designed and endorsed by a large partnership that included the outdoor recreation retail and manufacturing sector, the energy and automotive industries, private landowners, educational institutions, conservation organizations, sporting groups, and state and federal fish and wildlife agencies. Funding for species of conservation concern would come from existing mineral and energy royalties from federal lands. The bill garnered 110 cosponsors in the House of Representatives but was not acted upon. Stay tuned to see if the new Congress will reintroduce and pass this bill and how it will be implemented.

We like to call the birds of the Great Plains "our birds" because they represent our region, and perhaps it is good for us to take symbolic ownership of these animals that brighten our days, feed us, and guide us along paths and byways during our travels. Yes, the birds were here first, and the Great Plains has a wonderful diversity of colors, forms, sizes, and shapes of birds within its landscapes. The Great Plains is a dynamic place, and has been through the millennia. Humans continue to transform the plains today, and its future is in our hands.

If you are a fan of birds in the Great Plains, consider ways that you can support birds. Buy a Duck Stamp. Donate your time to a local nature center to help with wetland restoration, a prescribed burn, or their educational efforts for school kids. If you own land, spend time thinking about how the design of your property can be enhanced to accommodate birds and other wildlife. If you visit a wildlife refuge or other property, give the staff a pat on the back and put a few coins in the donation jar at the entrance to keep conservation programs funded. If you are thinking about college and you like birds and biology, consider a degree in conservation biology or wildlife management to make your own mark on the landscape. If you read about political issues that can affect our landscapes and the species that live in them, call your congressperson and tell them your story. In our own ways, we can all make a difference for the birds that call the Great Plains home.

CHAPTER FIVE

The Experience

Visiting the Birds of the Great Plains

Birds are all around us. While we celebrate their diversity, a birder can be overwhelmed with the task of identifying birds. If you are new to birding, the first step is to start looking for a few key characteristics as you watch a bird perched on a branch or even as it flies away from you. Keen birders develop skills to quickly note a list of features, known as "field marks." Still, the ability to catch field marks from a quick glimpse of a bird before it ducks into foliage or underwater can intimidate new birders. Grab a good book or app for your phone that provides bird identification as you leave for vacation or an excursion, and take time to flip through and familiarize yourself with the general order of the book or the logistics of the app. How do you find the hawks, ducks, or sparrows in your bird book? Many of the apps are designed to take a handful of field marks from that all-too-quick glance and suggest what species you may have seen, so practice to learn what information the app will need.

How to Begin to Identify Birds

You can easily start to distinguish a species of bird if you look for the following clues:

- *What was the general size and shape of the bird?* Compare it to common birds that you already know. Larger than a crow? About the size of a robin? Did it look like a duck?

- *What color is the bird?* A simple second step can help you narrow down the candidates for the bird that you encounter. Train your brain to think of comparison colors. Was it a brilliant yellow like a banana or a sunflower, or a dull yellow like a field of wheat? Was the bird a dark brown that reminded you of rich soil, or was it a light tan like a safari jacket?

- *Were the bird's wings solid in color or striped?* If you know the shape and color, the details of the wings can often bring you to a decision about which bird you saw. Some birds have light or dark stripes on their wings, called wing bars. In others the wings are a different color than the body, but solid in color. Some species, such as ducks, have a speculum, a brilliant patch of color on the upper surface of their outstretched wing, which can only be seen well when they fly. So, all is not lost when a bird flies away from you! Keep the binoculars on it to get additional clues.

- *Did you notice anything else unique about this bird?* Some birds have dark or light stripes near the eye. Some have stripes on their head or a crest of feathers. Others have chests that are spotted or striped. Some birds have pink legs and others have black legs. Some wading birds have yellow feet. Some birds have unusually shaped bills or beaks (figure 49). After you notice the basics of shape and coloration, look for details if you have time. And, again, watch the bird when it flies— some birds have colored tails or a white patch on the rump when they fly. You can evaluate the length of tail feathers compared to the rest of the body in flight.

- *Where are you?* Storms and migration seasons can affect where birds are found across continents, but the range maps shown in most bird identification guides should help you decide whether you should expect to find that species at your location. In addition to the range map, your bird book or app may note the typical habitat for birds you are considering. If you

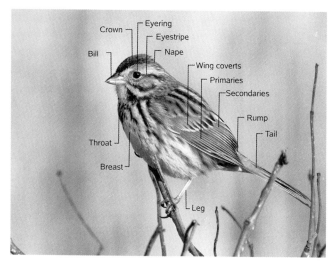

49. Parts of a bird and its plumage that may help when describing a bird to a fellow birder. USFWS photo of a song sparrow by Jim Hudgins, modified from color photo.

are watching birds in a wetland, that habitat narrows down the list of birds you might encounter. Similarly, grasslands and forests have their own communities of birds. The use of location and habitat can help narrow down the candidates as you look through your bird book.

With some practice, you can develop the skills needed to obtain useful field marks to locate an identification from a field guide of a bird you glimpsed quickly. An example of the ability to key on critical field marks can be seen in the unfinished, unidentified sketch of a "sparrow species" by Titian Ramsay Peale, an artist and naturalist who, in 1819, traveled with the Stephen Long expedition through the Great Plains on its way to the Rocky Mountains (figure 50). You can see how Peale noticed the eye stripe, brown cap, wing bars, and

50. Example of locating field marks of a bird quickly. *Top*, an unfinished sketch by Titian Ramsay Peale from 1820 (used with permission from the collection of the American Philosophical Society) to be compared with the photo of an American tree sparrow *at bottom* (photographer unknown).

even the lighter-colored lower bill, and these traits allow us to make a modern identification of this species as an American Tree Sparrow. Take a look at the sparrow pages in your bird book to confirm!

Responsibilities of a Birder

The British call them "twitchers," we call them "birders." Whatever the name you want to apply to yourself, stopping to look and listen for birds can add a unique dimension to any trip through the Great Plains and beyond. Even the authors of bird identification guides, such as David Sibley and the late Roger Tory Peterson, were once novice birders, so there is no reason to feel intimidated by the sport. Because of the joy and fascination with birding, the activity has become a multimillion-dollar industry in the United States. In 2011 the U.S. Fish and Wildlife Service estimated that there were forty-seven million bird watchers in the U.S., and eighteen million of those birders left home and went on the road to discover birds in new locations.

Birders spent $15 billion on their trips, and a further $26 billion on equipment, which seems to suggest the price of this book is a fairly good value! You do not need the fanciest of binoculars and spotting scopes to enjoy birding in the Great Plains. A simple pair of binoculars ranging from $50 to $200 is a good way to start, and your local sporting goods store should be able to help you with that purchase. However, the lure of getting better views of that gray-blob duck far out in the lake may drive you to consider a purchase of better optics sooner than you might predict. You will pay more for binoculars that have higher power to bring birds closer, better optics that allow tighter focus on small field marks, and lenses that allow more light to enter so you can expand your ventures into the low-light periods of dawn or dusk. An extra $500 may get in the name and logo of a famous optics company on your binoculars, but remember that you will need some cash for lunch on your trip. Cafés in the Great Plains serve wonderfully large tenderloin sandwiches and cherry pie.

In your travels, you may stumble upon birders who make you wonder how a human being can drift so far away from the mainstream—these are the folks with binoculars that cost more than the car that you are driving, and a camera with a lens longer than their walking stick. They are probably carrying a small notepad, and you may hear phrases such as "That's a new one for my life list," or "I'm pretty sure that one is a juvenile with an incomplete molt." You can learn a lot by talking to these intense birders, but do not expect this to be a long friendship. They are here for the birds. Do not expect all birders to know much about politics or current events, as some only use the internet to get updates from the Rare Bird Hotline.

Regardless of whether you keep a life list of birds or not, you are now one of the millions of birders in the U.S. Your newfound group has the potential to do a lot of good for the environment. When bird lovers join together in organizations such as the National Audubon Society or American Bird Conservancy, they can funnel membership funds to habitat protection or restoration projects. Audubon, for example, has forty-one nature centers on unique, member-purchased properties that preserve critical habitat in the United States, including five in the Great Plains. Members of these organizations in the Great Plains have been known to spend weekends harvesting wildflower seeds in prairie patches by hand so that proper restoration of prairie can be accomplished in the region. Groups of birders are often called upon to provide local protection for nests of endangered species or to assist with research projects that inform management decisions on state or federal lands.

However, birders also have the potential to be disruptive to birds, so we have to weigh the benefits of pushing just a little closer to get a better look against the downside of causing birds to flush from a nest or find a new perch site. Birds have higher average body temperatures and metabolism rates than we mammals, thus birds seem to be continuously foraging to maintain their energy levels. Causing them to waste energy is not a good thing. Nests without a parent on them are also more likely to be found by predators with a taste for eggs or nestlings, so we need to allow the parents to defend their nests and take care of their broods without interference. I recommend following these suggestions from the Code of Birding Ethics from the American Birding Association as you experience birds in the Great Plains:

- Avoid stressing birds or exposing them to danger, exercise restraint and caution during observation, photography, sound recording, or filming.
- Keep well back from nests and nesting colonies, roosts, display areas, and important feeding sites. In such sensitive areas, if there is a need for extended observation, photography, filming, or recording, try to use a blind or hide, and take advantage of natural cover.
- Stay on roads, trails, and paths where they exist; otherwise, keep habitat disturbance to a minimum.
- Do not enter private property without the owner's explicit permission.
- Respect the interests, rights, and skills of fellow birders, as well as people participating in other legitimate outdoor activities. Be especially helpful to beginning birders.
- During or after your trip, support the protection of important bird habitat through donations or your time.

Trials and Tribulations of Grassland Birding

Bird watchers in the Great Plains must be as persistent and resourceful as the birds for which they search. By definition,

51. A male dickcissel sings in a prairie in central Texas. Like many grassland birds, a dickcissel usually hides its black chin strap and a yellow eye-line and breast patch while foraging and flitting from perch to perch, only to expose them while singing and displaying to mark their territory. Photo by Isaac Sanchez.

plains are dominated by grasslands, and grasslands tend to enforce a selective advantage on birds that are camouflaged and brown. Quite simply, being brown helps to hide from predators. But an assortment of species of brown birds makes identification frustrating to bird watchers. We must keep looking for field marks, as the colored bits are tucked beneath chins, chests, and tails of many songbirds in the Great Plains (figure 51).

Grasslands are also large, lonely places for birds, which may cause disappointment among bird watchers who expect to walk out into the prairie to see a full symphony of birds. The key is to think like the birds—to find where they congregate, consider their wants and desires at different times of the year. Birds need to find each other to breed or before migration or for winter foraging, and bird watchers can tap into the same set of behaviors as well. The largest flocks of waterfowl in the northern plains are often seen as the birds stage to come south on key lakes in the region that have plenty of food to fuel migration. In the spring, similarly large flocks of ducks, geese, and sandhill cranes can be found at stopover points in the central and southern plains as they feed to fuel their northern migration. Likewise spring visits to lek sites of grouse will almost guarantee a sighting. The birds tend to use the same areas for dancing and booming each spring. I have coordinates of two greater prairie-chicken leks south of my home-town that I give to friends or visitors to my research lab. A few hours later, the adventurers return from a morning of fun observa-tions of the birds, and they admit that they really did not believe that I could guarantee that birds will be displaying at the same location near an intersection of two gravel roads year after year.

In addition to time of year and the annual cycles of the birds, an effective bird watcher should also consider habitat. The grass-lands of the Great Plains tend to have fewer species in a given location than forests or wetlands, because trees and water edges provide vertical structure for more niches, or spaces, for vari-ous species to exist. If your goal is a grassland bird such as the endemic Sprague's pipit or long-billed curlew, you must concen-trate on the low-diversity grasslands to find your quarry. But if your goal is a long list of birds seen, you must scurry to the tran-sition zones between grassland and other habitats. In the plains, avian biodiversity explodes at the edges of rivers, wetlands, or forest patches within grasslands. Birders call these areas *hotspots*, and they can be exciting locations for birding in the plains. For this reason, many of the suggested locations in this section are characterized by a mixture of habitats and bodies of water.

Where to Find Birds

You can easily throw a dart at a map of the Great Plains and find an interesting city, town, or village with a wonderful nat-ural area to explore. Birds will be there, and you would have a fine day. With any luck, there will be a small café that serves a delightfully tart rhubarb pie in the vicinity.

But in case you are opposed to living life in random fashion, I provide you with my choices for places to visit for excellent and unique birding experiences in the next pages. Some locations are personal favorites. A couple of them are local secrets. Other suggestions are constantly at the top of suggestions by groups like Audubon, The Nature Conservancy, Ducks Unlimited, or the Great Plains Ecotourism Coalition. You notice that many of the locations are public lands—owned and supported by the American taxpayer and open to all. Consider, as you visit the public lands on the list, voicing your support to your representatives in state legislatures and our federal Congress to keep public lands maintained and staffed. Future generations will thank you.

I have arranged the guide in sections starting with the Canadian provinces, moving down to the northern states of the plains in the U.S., and ending with the states of the southern plains. You can match the number on the map with the description of the destination. Planning a birding vacation? Consider looking for loops that you can make by connecting destinations of interest.

My students know that I have a thing about "sacred places"—not necessarily in a strict religious sense, but in a touch-the-soul sense. It does a body good to find quiet and reflect. In *Birding with Yeats: A Mother's Memoir*, Lynn Thompson wrote: "I think the most important quality in a bird watcher is a willingness to stand quietly and see what comes. Our everyday lives obscure a truth about existence— that at the heart of everything there lies a stillness and a light."

Indeed, see what comes. You will find birds, and sometimes birds will find you. I hope at least one psychologist with wings tilts its head to look you in the eye before hopping or flying away. But, most importantly, I hope you are able to use birds to find a sacred space. I guarantee it is possible at each and every one of the following locations.

ALBERTA
Official Bird: great-horned owl

1 Beaverhill Lake Nature Centre (east of Edmonton, near Tofield)

Why: The Nature Centre provides a nesting area for shorebirds and songbirds, and a migratory staging area for over 270 species of birds.

Habitats: Uplands: mix of mature aspen forest and grasslands; lake: extensive mud flats and marsh

Try to find: In the breeding season, observe from a distance the endangered piping plover; during migration, look for red-necked phalarope, pectoral sandpiper, dowitcher, black-bellied plover, semipalmated sandpiper, or American avocet

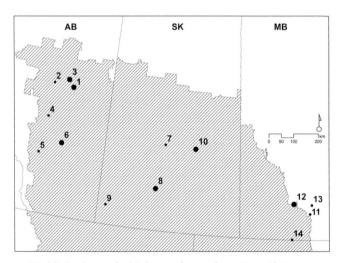

52. Highlighted areas for birding in the northern Great Plains (*hatched area*) in Canadian provinces. Numbers are associated with detailed descriptions following in the text. Larger symbols designate locations of especially high interest.

2 Clifford E. Lee Nature Sanctuary (southwest of Edmonton, near Devon)

Why: The sanctuary provides easy access to many habitats via trails and boardwalks with viewing platforms over the lake.

Habitats: A mix of sand hills, meadows, and aspen and pine woods, as well as marshes and lakes

Try to find: Visit during May to August to see breeding birds including ruffed grouse, three species of grebes, and many ducks and geese, as well as five species of woodpeckers and both red- and white-breasted nuthatch

3 Elk Island National Park (east of Edmonton, near Ardrossan)

Why: Elk Island features stunning scenery with a matrix of small hills with scattered wetlands with over eighty kilometers of trails; stretch your bird list to include big mammals—elk, moose, bison, and wood bison are in the park!

Habitats: Marsh, wetlands, sedge meadows, mixed forest, and aspen parkland

Try to find: Western tanager, downy woodpecker, great grey owl, northern hawk owl, ruffed grouse, American avocet, ruddy duck, and red-necked grebe

4 Gaetz Lakes Migratory Bird Sanctuary (Waskasoo Park; Red Deer, between Calgary and Edmonton)

Why: A migratory bird sanctuary since 1924, Gaetz Lakes offers 5 kilometers of trails, a bird blind, and a viewing deck in a variety of habitats.

Habitats: Mixed forest, lakes, and marshland

Try to find: Sora, pileated woodpecker, red-necked grebe

5 Inglewood Bird Sanctuary and Nature Center (Calgary)

Why: Inglewood is an urban reserve with an accessible nature center.

Habitats: Grasslands, mixed riverine forests

Try to find: Bald eagle, wood duck, mourning warbler, western-wood pewee, hairy woodpecker

6 Drumheller Valley (near Drumheller)

Why: A diversity of habitats from badlands to forest create a unique place for a day of birding; migratory raptors use the valley in the fall.

Habitats: Spruce forests, riverine woodlands, grasslands, and eroded badlands

Try to find: Tundra swan, rock wren, mountain bluebird, Say's phoebe, golden eagle, prairie falcon, and merlin

SASKATCHEWAN
Official Bird: sharp-tailed grouse

7 Bradwell National Wildlife Area (southeast of Saskatoon, near Bradwell)

Why: Bradwell features a series of restored and managed wetlands and grasslands that provide breeding habitat for waterfowl and shorebirds.

Habitats: Mixed-grass prairie, wetlands

Try to find: Horned grebe, bobolink, marbled godwit, Wilson's phalarope, and nesting waterfowl, including redhead and canvasback

8 Chaplin Lake (west of Regina, near Chaplin)

Why: Over 100,000 shorebirds stop to refuel on brine shrimp and other foods available in the saline wetland system of Chaplin Lake during their migration; the area is designated as one of five Canadian sites in the Western Hemispheric Shorebird Reserve Network.

Habitats: Saline lake, grasslands, marshland

Try to find: Northern pintail, American golden plover, piping plover, pectoral sandpiper, and semipalmated sandpiper

9 Cypress Hills Interprovincial Park (south of Maple Creek)

Why: Highly diverse habitats with trails and space and amenities are available to spend days or a short visit.

Habitats: Lodgepole pine and white spruce forests, wetlands, meadows, grasslands

Try to find: Red-naped sapsucker, common yellowthroat, Baltimore oriole, black tern, osprey, American white pelican, Caspian tern, bobolink

10 Quill Lakes International Bird Area (east of Saskatoon, near Wynyard)

Why: Visit Quill Lakes for the massive concentrations of ducks, geese, cranes, and shorebirds accessed through the Quill Lakes Interpretive Centre, the Wadena Wetlands Viewing Area, and the Foam Lake Heritage Marsh Viewing Area.

Habitats: Wetlands, lakes, grasslands

Try to find: Piping plover, eared grebe, marbled godwit, sandhill crane, black-crowned night heron, American avocet

MANITOBA

Official Bird: great grey owl

11 Assiniboine Park and Riparian Forest (Winnipeg)

Why: With an easily accessible riparian forest along the Assiniboine River, the park and forest are part of a corridor through Winnipeg.

Habitats: Open grasslands, English gardens, river-bottom forests

Try to find: During migration find yellow-bellied flycatcher, olive-sided flycatcher, Connecticut warbler, and mourning warbler; during the breeding season watch for wood duck, Cooper's hawk, great horned owl, great crested flycatcher, yellow-throated vireo, cliff swallow, and indigo bunting; in winter you might find Bohemian waxwing and white-winged crossbill

12 Delta Marsh (northwest of Winnipeg, near Portage la Prairie)

Why: Delta Marsh is an opportunity to see one of the world's great freshwater marshes with beaches and interpretive trails; the Delta Marsh Bird Observatory is the busiest banding station for songbirds in Canada. Throw a kayak or canoe in the water and paddle around to get up close and personal with the animals in the wetland system.

Habitats: Marshes, beach ridges

Try to find: Canvasback, yellow-headed blackbird, western grebe, Clark's grebe, Ross's goose, American white pelican, yellow warbler, Tennessee warbler, myrtle warbler

13 Oak Hammock Marsh Interpretive Center (north of Winnipeg, near Stonewall)

Why: This wildlife management area has thirty kilometers of trails as well as daily interpreter-led activities including paddling a voyageur canoe in the marsh; during migration the daily count of waterfowl can exceed four hundred thousand.

53. Delta Marsh (*right*) is located next to Lake Manitoba (*left*) and offers a variety of birding activities from open water to trails through marshlands. Photo provided by Ducks Unlimited Canada, used with permission.

Habitats: Prairie marshland, aspen-oak bluff, artesian springs, tall-grass prairie

Try to find: Yellow rail, Nelson's sparrow, Leconte's sparrow, American white pelican, marsh wren, Brewer's blackbird

14 **Pembina Valley Provincial Park (west of Reinland, just north of the Canada-U.S. border)**

Why: The park has trails, and the Pembina Valley offers rural roads between La Rivière and the park, with six wildlife management areas that provide more areas for bird watching.

Habitats: Small creeks, riparian forests, and shrublands

Try to find: Ruby-throated hummingbird, least flycatcher, eastern phoebe, yellow-throated vireo, red-eyed vireo, yellow warbler, American redstart, ovenbird, veery, bald eagle, and golden eagle

Northern Plains, United States

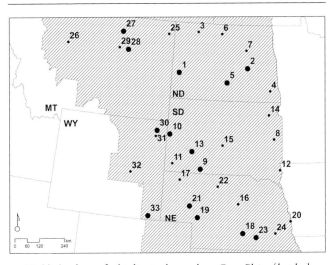

54. Highlighted areas for birding in the northern Great Plains (*hatched area*) in the United States. Numbers are associated with detailed descriptions following in the text. Larger symbols designate locations of especially high interest.

55. Landscape near the Talkington Trail in Theodore Roosevelt National Park, North Dakota. Photo by Matt Zimmerman.

NORTH DAKOTA

Official Bird: western meadowlark

1 Theodore Roosevelt National Park (near Belfield)

Why: Walk in the footsteps of our "conservation president" who ranched in the region, find a wide number of bird species in the Badlands region of North Dakota, and see elk and bison as well.

Habitats: Wooded flood plains, juniper woodland, and grassland

Try to find: Sharp-tailed grouse, northern harrier, burrowing owl, prairie falcon, Say's phoebe, black-billed magpie, eastern bluebird, mountain bluebird, black-and-white warbler, American redstart, yellow-breasted chat, grasshopper sparrow, spotted towhee, lazuli bunting, orchard oriole, Bullock's oriole, and Baltimore oriole

2 Arrowwood National Wildlife Refuge (north of Jamestown)

Why: Reserve a blind to watch sharp-tailed grouse males dance for females in the spring, or drive the auto route to see large numbers of migrating waterfowl. Chase Lake National Wildlife Refuge is about one hour to the west, adding another potential stop in a day of birding.

Habitats: Grasslands, wetlands, woodlands

Try to find: Sharp-tailed grouse, tundra swan, hooded merganser, northern harrier, upland sandpiper, marbled godwit, Wilson's phalarope, black tern, horned lark, American bittern, and Nelson's sparrow

3 Lostwood National Wildlife Refuge (north of Lostwood)

Why: This is an excellent place to view the Prairie Pothole wetland ecosystem with grassland birds and waterbirds; Des Lacs National Wildlife Refuge is one-half hour drive northeast of Lostwood NWR, providing another place to look for birds nearby.

Habitats: Mixed-grass prairie, pothole wetlands, alkaline lakes and marshes

Try to find: Piping plover, American avocet, sharp-tailed grouse, Sprague's pipit, Baird's sparrow, clay-colored sparrow, pied-billed grebe, horned grebe, eared grebe, willet, and Franklin's gull

4 Sheyenne National Grassland (southwest of Fargo, near Lisbon)

Why: This is the only national grassland in the tallgrass prairie region of the United States, and the home to the largest population of greater prairie-chickens in North Dakota.

Habitats: Tallgrass prairie, riparian forest

Try to find: Greater prairie-chicken, sharp-tailed grouse, northern harrier, upland sandpiper, marbled godwit, grasshopper sparrow, Le Conte's sparrow, dickcissel, bobolink, American woodcock, black-billed cuckoo, and pileated woodpecker

5 Long Lake National Wildlife Refuge (near Moffit)

Why: Sandhill Cranes stop at the refuge in the fall and shorebirds stop in the spring and late summer, and over twenty shorebird species might be seen in a single day; reserve a blind to watch grouse dance in the spring.

Habitats: Lake, marshland, mudflats, grasslands

Try to find: Sandhill crane, western grebe, Clark's grebe, American bittern, black-crowned night-heron, Virginia rail, sora, sharp-tailed grouse, northern harrier, and bobolink

6 J. Clark Salyer National Wildlife Refuge (north of Towner)

Why: Salyer is the largest refuge in North Dakota with large numbers of nesting waterfowl and a designated site in the Western Hemisphere Shorebird Reserve Network; an observation platform, driving routes, and trails allow access.

Habitats: Mixed-grass prairie, riparian woodland, marsh, sandhill grassland, and managed wetlands

Try to find: Sharp-tailed grouse, eared grebe, western grebe, American bittern, white-faced ibis, American avocet, Wilson's phalarope, sedge wren, marsh wren, Nelson's sparrow, rose-breasted grosbeak, orchard oriole, Sprague's pipit, chestnut-collared longspur, grasshopper sparrow, Baird's sparrow, and clay-colored sparrow

7 Sullys Hill National Game Preserve (east of Fort Totten, on the south shore of Devil's Lake)

Why: Varied habitats in the Prairie Pothole region are home to over 250 species of migratory birds and waterfowl as well as bison, elk, and prairie dogs.

Habitats: Richly forested hills, wetlands, and prairie grasslands

Try to find: Wood duck, hooded merganser, sharp-tailed grouse, double-crested cormorant, American white pelican, black-crowned night-heron, yellow-bellied sapsucker, yellow-throated vireo, ovenbird, black-and-white warbler, American redstart, eastern towhee, rose-breasted grosbeak, and Baltimore oriole

SOUTH DAKOTA
Official Bird: ring-necked pheasant

8 Oakwood Lakes State Park (northwest of Brookings)

Why: This state park in the glacial lakes region is best known for flocks of migrating waterfowl.

Habitats: Open water, marsh, woodland, grassland

Try to find: Pied-billed grebe, great blue heron, great egret, green heron, warbling vireo, cedar waxwing, yellow warbler, and Baltimore oriole

56. Trumpeter swans and other waterfowl at Lacreek National Wildlife Refuge, South Dakota. Photo by Tom Koerner, USFWS.

9 Lacreek National Wildlife Refuge (near Martin)

Why: A series of managed wetlands provide for great views of waterfowl, marsh birds, and shorebirds, especially during migration.

Habitats: Grasslands, wetlands

Try to find: Trumpeter swan, blue-winged teal, northern pintail, American bittern, American avocet, willet, Wilson's snipe, Wilson's phalarope, burrowing owl, sharp-tailed grouse, upland sandpiper, marbled godwit, loggerhead shrike, and Bell's vireo

10 Black Hills, Spearfish Canyon (north of Rapid City, near Spearfish)

Why: The Black Hills regions is an island of unique habitat in the midst of the Great Plains, resembling the Rocky Mountains; the Spearfish Canyon Scenic Byway is a unique way to look for birds.

Habitats: Ponderosa pine and spruce forests

Try to find: American dipper, ruffed grouse, white-throated swift, red-naped sapsucker, dusky flycatcher, Cordilleran flycatcher, violet-green swallow, red-breasted nuthatch, canyon wren, mountain bluebird, MacGillivray's warbler, western tanager, black-headed grosbeak, pine siskin, American three-toed woodpecker, Townsend's solitaire, and red crossbill

11 Black Hills, Cascade Springs (south of Hot Spring)

Why: Paved trails provide access to the springs for a quick and rewarding stop.

Habitats: Riparian woodland, juniper shrub

Try to find: White-throated swift, Townsend's solitaire, Wilson's snipe, lazuli bunting, yellow-breasted chat, northern harrier, mountain bluebird, marsh wren, Bullock's oriole, chipping sparrow, red-breasted nuthatch, and pine siskin

12 **Newton Hills State Park (south of Sioux Falls)**

Why: The rugged, forested terrain provides nesting birds that are rare elsewhere in South Dakota; the site is used heavily by songbirds during migration.

Habitats: Deciduous forest, tallgrass prairie

Try to find: American woodcock, barred owl, eastern whip-poor-will, yellow-bellied sapsucker, yellow-throated vireo, blue-gray gnatcatcher, wood thrush, blue-winged warbler, eastern towhee, scarlet tanager, yellow-billed cuckoo, black-billed cuckoo, rose-breasted grosbeak, indigo bunting, orchard oriole, and Baltimore oriole

13 **Badlands National Park (south of Wall)**

Why: The Badlands landscape is unique in the Great Plains, and the bare ground in prairie dog towns and eroded, geological spaces provides unusual niches for birds.

Habitats: Cliffs, grasslands, eroded land, juniper woodland

Try to find: Sharp-tailed grouse, northern harrier, upland sandpiper, long-billed curlew, marbled godwit, burrowing owl, loggerhead shrike, horned lark, grasshopper sparrow, golden eagle, ferruginous hawk, white-throated swift, prairie falcon, Say's phoebe, black-billed magpie, rock wren, mountain bluebird, blue grosbeak, and orchard oriole

14 **Waubay National Wildlife Refuge (north of Waubay)**

Why: In the Lakota Sioux language, "Waubay" refers to a place where a number of birds make their nests. Established as a refuge in 1935, here you can find more than 100 species of breeding birds and an additional 140 species during migration.

Habitats: Mixture of large and small glacially created lakes, ponds, and wetlands, grassland uplands, woodlands

Try to find: Red-necked grebe, western grebe, American bittern, upland sandpiper, marbled godwit, Wilson's phalarope, Franklin's gull, black tern, Forster's tern, red-bellied woodpecker, marsh wren, grasshopper sparrow, bobolink, and yellow-headed blackbird

15 Fort Pierre National Grassland (south of Pierre, South Dakota)
Why: This is a large area with little development as far as the eye can see; in the spring, make a reservation to watch greater prairie-chicken perform their mating dances.

Habitats: Grassland

Try to find: Sharp-tailed grouse, northern harrier, upland sandpiper, marbled godwit, Wilson's phalarope, burrowing owl, short-eared owl, horned lark, grasshopper sparrow, lark bunting, dickcissel, and bobolink; in winter: golden eagle, rough-legged hawk, gyrfalcon, northern shrike, Lapland longspur

NEBRASKA
Official Bird: western meadowlark

16 Calamus Reservoir State Recreation Area and Wildlife Management Area (northwest of Burwell)
Why: A large reservoir attracts bald eagles and American white pelicans in the spring; a local prairie-chicken festival is held each April, and you can extend your birding by driving or walking along Pebble Creek Road and Windy Hill Road north of Burwell for a unique mix of topography and habitats along the North Loup River.

Habitats: Sandhills grasslands, cedar groves, riparian forest

Try to find: American white pelican, greater prairie-chicken, sharp-tailed grouse (keep your eyes peeled for hybrid chicken-grouse), bald eagle, grasshopper sparrow, northern bobwhite, red-headed woodpecker, Bell's vireo

17 Chadron State Park and Sowbelly Canyon (west of Chadron)

Why: The Pine Ridge landscape provides Nebraska with a taste of bird species associated with the Rocky Mountains; Sow Belly Canyon is accessed by road starting a half mile north of the town of Harrison; drive east on Sowbelly Road and then north to enter Sowbelly Canyon (watch for bighorn sheep as a bonus).

Habitats: Ponderosa pine forests, grasslands

Try to find: Common poorwill, white-throated swift, Lewis's woodpecker, western wood-pewee, Cordilleran flycatcher, Say's phoebe, pinyon jay, violet-green swallow, pygmy nuthatch, rock wren, mountain bluebird, western tanager

18 Platte River Valley/Rowe Sanctuary (east of Kearney, near Gibbon)

Why: The migration of sandhill cranes provides one of the best spectacles of wildlife in North America from mid-February to early April. Over 400,000 cranes stop to refuel along the Platte River Valley. Rowe Sanctuary offers a free nature center, and there are nearby places to view cranes in the evening when they gather to roost in the Platte River and in the morning as they depart. During the day, drive gravel back roads long the southern edge of the Platte River between Fort Kearney State Recreation Area and Doniphan to search for a whooping crane in the midst of foraging sandhill cranes. A crane festival is held in mid-March.

Habitats: Riparian cottonwood and red-cedar forests, grasslands, crop fields

Try to find: Sandhill crane, whooping crane, snow geese in the spring; during breeding season find upland sandpiper, least tern, belted kingfisher, willow flycatcher, bobolink, Baltimore oriole, orchard oriole

19 Lake McConaughy/Lake Ogallala (north of Ogallala)

Why: Lake McConaughy is Nebraska's largest body of water and is fed by the North Platte River. The spillway flows into Lake Ogallala (created to dig the dam for the larger lake). The confluence of southern, Sandhills, western, and riparian regions provides a unique mix of species in summer, but birders flock during migration and in winter to see unique waterbirds.

Habitats: Riparian forests, Sandhills grassland, lakes, marshland, mudflats

Try to find: In the winter, bald eagles, ring-billed gull, herring gull, common loon, western grebe, tundra swan, and the rarer list of Sabine's gull, mew gull, Iceland gull, glaucous-winged gull; during breeding season, view from a distance the protected nests of piping plover and least tern

20 Fontenelle Forest Nature Center (south of Omaha)

Why: A mix of habitats with trails and a wetland observation platform makes the nature center an easily accessible area for urban birders.

Habitats: Bottomland forest, oak savannah, grassland, wetlands

Try to find: Red-shouldered hawk, pileated woodpecker, Acadian flycatcher, Carolina wren, prothonotary warbler, cerulean warbler, Kentucky warbler, yellow-throated warbler, summer tanager, cinnamon teal, Couch's kingbird, spotted towhee, black-headed grosbeak, lazuli bunting

21 Crescent Lake National Wildlife Refuge (north of Oshkosh)

Why: Only the dedicated make the thirty-mile trek on unpaved roads to reach this large refuge, and you will be rewarded with a unique Sandhills landscape and a fun day of birding.

Habitats: Sandhills grassland, freshwater and alkaline ponds and wetlands

Try to find: In addition to many ducks, find pied-billed grebe, eared grebe, western grebe, American white pelican, American bittern, white-faced ibis, black-necked stilt, American avocet, willet, upland sandpiper, long-billed curlew, Wilson's phalarope, sharp-tailed grouse, burrowing owl, loggerhead shrike, horned lark

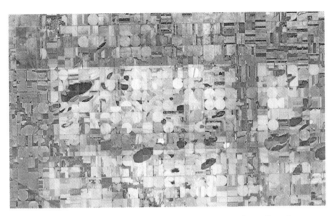

57. The landscape of the Rainwater Basin region is dotted with wetlands in a matrix of farm fields. Clay Center, Nebraska, is in the *upper left*, and circular patterns are caused by irrigation with center-pivot systems.

22 Valentine National Wildlife Refuge (south of Valentine)

Why: You've decided to take the back roads to the Black Hills, so why not stop and investigate the thirty-six natural, long, narrow lakes in the midst of the rolling dunes of the Sandhills region? This is one of the few places that greater prairie-chickens and sharp-tailed grouse can both be seen.

Habitats: Lakes, ponds, marshland, Sandhills grassland, red-cedar groves

Try to find: Eared grebe, western grebe, pied-billed grebe, northern shoveler, blue-wing teal, Wilson's snipe, American avocets, long-billed curlew, upland sandpiper, and Swainson's hawk

23 Rainwater Basin wetlands (near Clay Center)

Why: The large region of rain-fed wetlands in south-central Nebraska is largely unknown outside of the state, and it is one of the most important stopover sites during spring migration in the Central Flyway for waterfowl, shorebirds, and marsh birds. More than sixty managed areas (each with parking lots and access points for hiking, hunting, and birding) for waterfowl production in thirteen counties make up this wetland complex. Wise birders do not lose sight of the uplands and crop fields surrounding each wetland, as well—many migrating shore birds prefer to use unplanted soybean fields in the spring.

Habitats: Wetland, mudflats, open water, crop fields, grasslands, small woodlands

Try to find: A tree. No, just kidding. But seriously, you should try. For birds, look for whooping crane, double-crested cormorant, American white pelican, buff-breasted sandpiper, northern pintail, northern shoveler, northern harrier, least bittern, and great-tailed grackle.

24 Spring Creek Prairie Audubon Center (west of Lincoln)

Why: You will find this an easily accessed tract of tallgrass prairie in a rolling landscape along the Oregon Trail with three miles of trails.

Habitats: Tallgrass prairie, ponds, wetland, woodland

Try to find: Greater prairie-chicken, northern bobwhite, upland sandpiper, grasshopper sparrow, Henslow's sparrow, dickcissel, bobolink; in winter, northern harrier, rough-legged hawk, northern shrike, Sprague's pipit, Smith's longspur, Le Conte's sparrow, Harris's sparrow

MONTANA
Official Bird: western meadowlark

25 Medicine Lake National Wildlife Refuge (north of Culbertson)

Why: Explore the western edge of the Prairie Pothole region with many small wetlands that reward the curious birder; stop at an overlook to see a nesting colony of up to ten thousand American white pelicans, or reserve a spot in a viewing blind to watch sharp-tailed grouse dance in the spring.

Habitats: Marshes, shelterbelts, croplands, grasslands, large water bodies

Try to find: Sprague's pipit, northern harriers, western grebes, Swainson's hawk, ferruginous hawk, American avocet, marbled godwit, upland sandpiper, burrowing owl, chestnut-collared longspur, grasshopper sparrow, Baird's sparrow, bobolink, yellow-headed blackbird

26 Benton Lake National Wildlife Refuge (north of Great Falls)

Why: The focus of your visit is a large wetland created by glaciers, but the location on the western edge of the Great Plains, surrounded on three sides by mountains, results in a large number of species of birds for visitors.

Habitats: Wetland, grassland

Try to find: Sharp-tailed grouse, eared grebe, western grebe, American white pelican, black-crowned night-heron, white-faced ibis, sora, black-necked stilt, American avocet, Wilson's phalarope, Franklin's gull, black tern, common tern, Forster's tern, long-billed curlew, burrowing owl, short-eared owl, loggerhead shrike, Sprague's pipit

27 Bowdoin National Wildlife Refuge (east of Malta)

Why: The Missouri River now is over seventy miles away, but the refuge's lake was once a part of the Missouri River during preglacial times. Approximately six thousand acres of wetlands are set in a matrix of grassland to provide a diverse mix of habitats for your visit.

Habitats: Saline and freshwater wetlands, native prairie, shrubland

Try to find: Canada goose, gadwall, American wigeon, canvasback, redhead, ruddy duck, white-faced ibis, common tern, black tern, long-billed curlew, greater sage-grouse, sharp-tailed grouse, short-eared owl, Sprague's pipit, chestnut-collared longspur, grasshopper sparrow, Baird's sparrow, lark bunting, vesper sparrow, bobolink

58. Sharp-tailed grouse rest on a lekking area near the auto tour route at the Charles M. Russell National Wildlife Refuge, Montana. Photo by Katie Theule, U S F W S.

28 Charles M. Russell National Wildlife Refuge (south of Glasgow)

Why: On the banks of Fort Peck Lake along the route traveled by Lewis and Clark, your stop can include sightings of elk, mule deer, pronghorn, bighorn sheep, sage- and sharp-tailed grouse, or bald eagles

Habitats: Badlands, cottonwood river bottoms, forested coulees, sagebrush steppes, mixed-grass prairies

Try to find: Sage-grouse, sharp-tailed grouse, McCown's long-spur, chestnut-collared longspur, long-billed curlew, mountain plover, burrowing owl, spotted towhee, green-tailed towhee, western tanager, lazuli bunting, eastern kingbird, western kingbird

29 American Prairie Reserve (south of Malta)

Why: Take in scenic overlooks, bison, and a host of grassland birds on lands accumulated by this private reserve near Charles M. Russell National Wildlife Refuge.

Habitats: Grassland, ponds, streams, wetlands

Try to find: Burrowing owl, snowy owl, ferruginous hawk, Swainson's hawk, prairie falcon, peregrine falcons, gray partridge, greater sage-grouse, ring-necked pheasant, sharp-tailed grouse, wild turkey, Barrow's goldeneye, cinnamon teal, hooded merganser, tundra swan, wood duck

WYOMING

Official Bird: western meadowlark

30 Devils Tower National Monument (southwest of Hulett)

Why: You'll find a rewarding birding area at one of the top geologic destinations in the United States. The nine-hundred-foot Devils Tower is a dramatic part of the landscape, and its rock columns also serve as a nesting site for prairie falcons.

Habitats: Ponderosa pine forest, grassland, cottonwood riverine forest

Try to find: Golden eagle, peregrine falcon, white-throated swift, Lewis's woodpecker, red-headed woodpecker, western wood-pewee, Say's phoebe, plumbeous vireo, pinyon jay, black-billed magpie, violet-green swallow, cliff swallow, red-breasted

59. A variety of habitats are available for birding in the shadow of the tower at Devils Tower National Monument, Wyoming. Photo by Russell Feldhausen.

nuthatch, rock wren, mountain bluebird, Townsend's solitaire, yellow warbler, yellow-rumped warbler, spotted towhee, western tanager, black-headed grosbeak, lazuli bunting, red crossbill

31 Keyhole State Park (northeast of Moorcroft)

Why: A birding destination so good that researchers come here to band birds. The combination of habitats near a large reservoir creates a large diversity of birds to be found at any time of year.

Habitats: Large reservoir, grasslands, woodland, mudflats

Try to find: Western grebe, American white pelican, American avocet, upland sandpiper, western wood-pewee, western kingbird, eastern kingbird, black-billed magpie, horned lark, mountain bluebird, yellow warbler, Brewer's sparrow, lark sparrow, vesper sparrow; in migration, find common loon among the ducks

32 Edness Kimball Wilkins State Park (east of Casper)

Why: Bring a picnic and enjoy this site for the day.

Habitats: Cottonwood riverine forest, ponds

Try to find: Wood duck, mallard, blue-winged teal, common merganser, double-crested cormorant, American white pelican, great blue heron, bald eagle, least flycatcher, warbling vireo, tree swallow, yellow warbler, lark sparrow, black-headed grosbeak, Bullock's oriole, long-eared owl, wood thrush, hooded warbler

33 Lions Park (northern Cheyenne)

Why: This urban park, surrounding Sloan Lake, ranks as one of Wyoming's top birding spots for species lists.

Habitats: Lake, cottonwoods

Try to find: Osprey, western grebe, black-crowned night-heron, belted kingfisher, yellow warbler, yellow-headed blackbird, Townsend's solitaire, common loon, white-faced ibis, MacGillivray's warbler, chestnut-sided warbler, chipping sparrow, clay-colored sparrow

Southern Plains, United States

KANSAS

Official Bird: western meadowlark

1 Flint Hills National Wildlife Refuge (southeast of Emporia)

Why: Make an easy day-trip from Kansas City to experience the results of intensive management of wetlands and grassland for restoration purposes.

Habitats: Grassland, wetland, forests

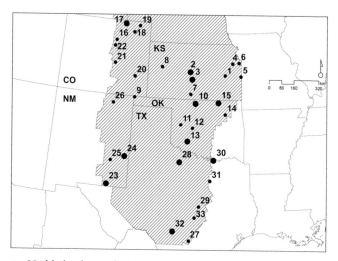

60. Highlighted areas for birding in the southern Great Plains (*hatched area*). Numbers are associated with detailed descriptions following in the text. Larger symbols designate locations of especially high interest.

> *Try to find:* Pileated woodpecker, greater prairie-chicken, yellow-billed cuckoo, horned lark, warbling vireo, blue-gray gnatcatcher

2 Cheyenne Bottoms Wildlife Area (northeast of Great Bend)

> *Why:* This area is a critical stopover during migration for shorebirds; almost the entire population of stilt sandpiper and Baird's sandpiper rest here on migration. That is pretty cool.
>
> *Habitats:* Grasslands and open and vegetated pools with a variety of depths
>
> *Try to find:* American bittern, least bittern, white-faced ibis, black tern, burrowing owl, Neotropic cormorant; during migration, sandhill crane, whooping crane, peregrine falcon

61. Quivira National Wildlife Refuge, Kansas, is a popular destination for those searching for the elusive, endangered whooping crane. Photo by Dan Severson, USFWS.

3 Quivira National Wildlife Refuge (southeast of Great Bend)

Why: A five-mile auto tour route gets you close to the action at an important migratory stopover for thousands of birds each year. Combine a trip to Cheyenne Bottoms for a thrilling day of birding during migration.

Habitats: Marshes, ponds, grasslands, woodlands

Try to find: Redhead, Neotropic cormorant, black rail, snowy plover, Wilson's phalarope, least tern, black tern, marsh wren, yellow-headed blackbird, Mississippi kite, upland sandpiper, scissor-tailed flycatcher, painted bunting

4 Clinton Lake, Clinton State Park (southwest of Lawrence)

Why: The large lake is an easy access in eastern Kansas, with a potential bird list of over 250 species.

Habitats: Open lake, marshes, woodland

Try to find: Red-headed woodpecker, scissor-tailed flycatcher, eastern bluebird, prothonotary warbler, painted bunting, American white pelican, bald eagle, osprey, Franklin's gull

5 Marais des Cygnes Wildlife Area, National Wildlife Refuge (north of Pleasanton)

Why: A state wildlife area and a national wildlife refuge, both named "marsh of the swans," combine to give a good show.

Habitats: Bottomland hardwood forest, marshes, open impoundments, grassland

Try to find: American white pelican, bald eagle, northern bobwhite, wild turkey, red-shouldered hawk, scissor-tailed flycatcher, loggerhead shrike, fish crow, prothonotary warbler, yellow-throated warbler, grasshopper sparrow, and dickcissel

6 Shawnee Mission Park (Shawnee)

Why: Experience an urban birding experience that is a local hotspot; come in the spring and fall to avoid the summer crush of people and maximize the number of birds.

Habitats: Forest, grassland, open lake

Try to find: Wild turkey, great blue heron, green heron, red-tailed hawk, yellow-billed cuckoo, western kingbird, scissor-tailed flycatcher, warbling vireo, Louisiana waterthrush, northern parula, summer tanager, orchard oriole, Baltimore oriole

7 Gypsum Hills Wildlife Drive (from Hardtner to Sun City)

Why: This high-diversity auto tour route is perfect for a winter birding trip through the buttes and hills of the Red Hills (or Gypsum Hills) region; or, take a bike! Go west of Hardtner on Central Avenue/Hackberry Road, after nineteen miles turn right on Aetna Road, jog left/west on U.S. 160 for a mile and finish by going seven miles north to Sun City.

Habitats: Mixed grass prairie, red-cedar thickets

Try to find: In the winter, mountain bluebirds, American robins, cedar waxwings, Townsend's solitaires

8 **Lake Scott State Park (north of Scott City)**

Why: Explore a mix of eastern and western species in the Great Plains hybrid zone.

Habitats: Open lake, riparian cottonwoods, rocky bluffs

Try to find: Mississippi kite, eastern screech-owl, Say's phoebe, western kingbird, eastern kingbird, rock wren, black-headed grosbeak, western meadowlark, Bullock's oriole, Baltimore oriole

OKLAHOMA
Official Bird: scissor-tailed flycatcher

9 **Black Mesa Preserve (northwest of Boise City)**

Why: The Rocky Mountains meet the shortgrass prairie, and The Nature Conservancy's preserve offers a four-hour (round trip) hike to the peak of Black Mesa with some excellent birding along the way.

Habitats: Juniper/shrub oak, juniper/pinyon woodland, short-grass prairie

Try to find: Golden eagles, scaled quail, black-billed magpie, pinyon jay, greater roadrunner, black-chinned hummingbird, ladder-backed woodpecker, vermilion flycatcher, Chihuahuan raven, common raven, curve-billed thrasher, canyon towhee, Cassin's sparrow, black-throated sparrow

10 **Salt Plains National Wildlife Refuge (east of Cherokee)**

Why: The landscape may look like a moonscape, but it is home to two species of conservation concern, the interior least tern and western snowy plover. The salt flats foster salt brine flies that provide a smorgasbord to the local waterbirds.

Habitats: 11,200-acre salt flat

Try to find: Double-crested cormorant, snowy egret, tricolored heron, white-faced ibis, Mississippi kite, black-necked stilt, greater roadrunner, western kingbird, scissor-tailed flycatcher, painted bunting, dickcissel

11 Washita National Wildlife Refuge (northwest of Clinton)

Why: A large lake surrounded by grasslands and croplands attracts a variety of wintering waterbirds.

Habitats: Rolling prairie, woodlands, farm fields, mud flats, marshes, open water

Try to find: In winter, sandhill crane, Canada goose, snow goose, Ross's goose, greater white-fronted goose, mallard, American wigeon, gadwall, northern pintail, ring-necked duck, redhead, hooded merganser

12 Red Rock Canyon State Park (south of Hinton)

Why: Come for the red-rock canyon and stay for the birds.

Habitats: Scrub oaks, junipers, riparian forests

Try to find: Greater roadrunner, great crested flycatcher, eastern phoebe, rough-winged swallow, Carolina wren, canyon wren, wood thrush, black-and-white warbler, prairie warbler, summer tanager, indigo bunting, painted bunting, Chuck-will's-widow, black-capped vireo, blue grosbeak

13 Wichita Mountains Wildlife Refuge (northwest of Lawton)

Why: Take in a long list of bird species while having an opportunity to see restorations of bison, elk, prairie dogs, and river otters.

Habitats: Mixed-grass prairie, oak forests, granite formations, open lakes

Try to find: Mississippi kite, greater roadrunner, burrowing owl, black-chinned hummingbird, scissor-tailed flycatcher, cave swallow, rock wren, canyon wren, Bewick's wren, Cassin's sparrow, grasshopper sparrow, rufous-crowned sparrow

62. Visitors can explore stunning landscapes at Wichita Mountains Wildlife Refuge, Oklahoma. Photo by Jonathan Wheeler.

14 Mohawk Park/Oxley Nature Center (Tulsa)

Why: Go golfing or check out the zoo in this city park after you cruise woodland trails for spring migrants.

Habitats: Wetlands, grassland, woodland, open lake

Try to find: Red-shouldered hawk, pileated woodpecker, prothonotary warbler, yellow-throated warbler, summer tanager, Mississippi kite, broad-winged hawk, great horned owl, barred owl, scissor-tailed flycatcher, painted bunting

15 Tallgrass Prairie Preserve (north of Pawhuska)

Why: Get lost on miles of roads or trails through tallgrass prairie, or reduce that chance by picking up a map before you explore. Also, watch out for bison.

Habitats: Tallgrass prairie

Try to find: Greater prairie-chicken, scissor-tailed flycatcher, dickcissel, northern bobwhite, wild turkey, upland sandpiper, loggerhead shrike, Bell's vireo, grasshopper sparrow, Henslow's sparrow, painted bunting

COLORADO
Official Bird: lark bunting

16 Barr Lake State Park (northeast of Denver)

Why: This 1,900-acre lake attracts migrating waterfowl and shore-birds and is accessible by nearby interstates and the Denver airport. Although dwarfed by the lake, the park also has seven hundred acres of grasslands.

Habitats: Open lake, mudflats, grassland, cottonwood forest

Try to find: Bald eagle, American white pelican, white-faced ibis, American avocet, burrowing owl, prairie falcon, Say's phoebe, warbling vireo, horned lark, lark sparrow, lark bunting, blue grosbeak, lazuli bunting, yellow-headed blackbird, and orchard oriole

17 Pawnee National Grassland (northeast of Greeley)

Why: Get away from it all on unpaved roads in large open grasslands.

Habitats: Prairie and interspersed private farmland

Try to find: Golden eagle, Swainson's hawk, ferruginous hawk, mountain plover, burrowing owl, prairie falcon, Say's phoebe, horned lark, chestnut-collared longspur, McCown's longspur, Cassin's sparrow, grasshopper sparrow, Brewer's sparrow, lark sparrow, lark bunting, vesper sparrow, and Bullock's oriole

18 Prewitt Reservoir State Wildlife Area (south of Merino)

Why: Walk trails to look for passerines or scan the lake for migrating waterbirds and shorebirds. The area is a haven during fall and spring migration.

Habitats: Riparian forests, open lake, mudflats

Try to find: During fall migration, dabbling ducks, short-billed dowitcher, buff-breasted sandpiper, peregrine falcon, Sabine's gull, Franklin's gull, black tern, Caspian tern

19 Tamarack Ranch State Wildlife Area (northeast of Sterling)

Why: This linear public area along the South Platte River provides a variety of habitat that attracts a full suite of regional landbirds.

Habitats: Grassland, river channels, riparian forest, hedgerows

Try to find: During winter, white-throated sparrow, Harris's sparrows; during summer, ring-necked pheasant, Bell's vireo, yellow-breasted chat, blue grosbeak, field sparrow, eastern towhee, spotted towhee, northern cardinal, and Baltimore oriole

20 John Martin Reservoir State Park (west of Lamar)

Why: A busy reservoir attracts waterfowl and waterbirds, while grasslands often attract unique, vagrant songbirds.

Habitats: Open water, riparian forest, grasslands

Try to find: During migration, grebes, American white pelican, shorebirds, gulls, and terns; during summer, piping plover, least tern, scaled quail, ring-necked pheasant, greater roadrunner, burrowing owl, red-bellied woodpecker, loggerhead shrike, horned lark, rock wren, and eastern bluebird; during winter, golden eagle and bald eagle

21 Fountain Creek Regional Park (north of Fountain)

Why: Trails and a nature center make this a nice stop for migrant songbirds, including thirty species of warblers.

Habitats: Riparian forests, ponds, creek

Try to find: Near ponds, Virginia rail and sora; in summer, black-chinned hummingbird, broad-tailed hummingbird, belted kingfisher, western wood-pewee, Say's phoebe, western kingbird, eastern kingbird, lazuli bunting, Bullock's oriole; during migration, Swainson's warbler, Cape May warbler, Blackburnian warbler

22 Cherry Creek State Park (Denver)

Why: This urban park boasts a bird list of over three hundred species. Birders often find rare waterbirds, gulls, and songbirds in and around an 880-acre reservoir.

Habitats: Creeks, woodland, open water, grassland, marshes

Try to find: Burrowing owl, double-crested cormorant, American white pelican, thirty species of shorebirds, bald eagle; in fall, osprey; in winter, rough-legged hawk, ferruginous hawk, and northern shrike

63. Scattered trees surround a marsh at Cherry Creek State Park, Colorado.

NEW MEXICO
Official Bird: roadrunner

23 Carlsbad Caverns National Park/Rattlesnake Springs (south of Carlsbad)

Why : Come for the cave at Carlsbad, and stay for birding at Rattlesnake Springs with a bird list of over three hundred species in an oasis in the Chihuahuan Desert.

Habitats: Seasonal wetland, spring, riparian forest, scrubland

Try to find: During migration, rare species such as Williamson's sapsucker, blue-headed vireo, and worm-eating warbler; during breeding season, gray hawk, wild turkey, yellow-billed cuckoo, black-chinned hummingbird, black phoebe, Say's phoebe, vermilion flycatcher, ash-throated flycatcher, Bell's vireo, Lucy's warbler, yellow-breasted chat, summer tanager, pyrrhuloxia, and painted bunting

24 Milnesand Prairie Preserve (north of Milnesand)

Why: You will enjoy a 28,000-acre reserve with high-quality habitat that attracts ground-nesting birds. More than fifty leks of lesser prairie-chicken dot the reserve. Visit during the spring for their prairie-chicken festival.

Habitats: Unfragmented grassland, oak shrubland

Try to find: Lesser prairie-chickens, burrowing owls, scaled quail, Cassin's sparrow, and grasshopper sparrow

25 Bitter Lake National Wildlife Refuge (northeast of Roswell)

Why: Pick a time of year, and you will find something exciting here. It is underrated as a birding destination, so you may have the run of the place. Check out the auto tour route.

Habitats: Grasslands, sand dunes, brushy bottomlands, open water

Try to find: During migration, American white pelican, osprey, greater yellowlegs, lesser yellowlegs, western sandpiper, and long-billed dowitcher; over winter, great flocks of geese, ducks, and sandhill cranes; during breeding season, blue-winged teal, cinnamon teal, black-necked stilt, American avocet, least tern, snowy plover, scaled quail, white-faced ibis, Virginia rail, Wilson's phalarope, greater roadrunner, Cassin's sparrow, pyrrhuloxia, and blue grosbeak

26 **Maxwell National Wildlife Refuge (Maxwell)**

Why: This refuge is an iconic, easy-to-access hotspot with many types of habitat and several prairie dog towns within view of the Sangre de Cristo Mountains.

Habitats: Grassland, open water, wetlands, cropland, small woodlands

Try to find: In the fall, geese, ducks, sandhill cranes, golden eagle, bald eagle, rough-legged hawk, and ferruginous hawk; in winter, prairie falcon, northern shrike, mountain bluebird, longspurs, and American tree sparrow; during breeding season, burrowing owl, American avocet, Wilson's phalarope, cinnamon teal, ruddy duck, pied-billed grebe, eared grebe, western grebe, Clark's grebe, white-faced ibis, long-billed curlew, horned lark, Cassin's sparrow, grasshopper sparrow, lark bunting, vesper sparrow, savannah sparrow, blue grosbeak, yellow-headed blackbird, and lesser goldfinch

TEXAS

Official Bird: northern mockingbird

27 **Mitchell Lake Audubon Center (San Antonio)**

Why: This urban delight with 1,200 acres includes a 600-acre lake and 200 acres of wetlands. A centerpiece for the Audubon Center includes several former wastewater treatment ponds that are now heavily used by shorebirds from late summer through winter.

Habitats: Open water, wetlands, ponds, grasslands, woodland

Try to find: During migration, black-bellied whistling-duck, least grebe, Neotropic cormorant, anhinga, American white pelican, roseate spoonbill, and black-necked stilt; breeding birds include greater roadrunner, groove-billed ani, black-chinned hummingbird, golden-fronted woodpecker, ladder-backed woodpecker, crested caracara, ash-throated flycatcher, brown-crested flycatcher, scissor-tailed flycatcher, cave swallow, verdin, long-billed thrasher, orchard oriole, and Bullock's oriole

28 Wichita Loop (between Seymour and Wichita Falls)

Why: Two city parks, a state park, and a private ranch provide an assortment of birding opportunities in a short loop drive through the mesquite plains country. To take the drive, start in Lucy Park, in Wichita Falls. Then head for Lake Arrowhead State Park by leaving Wichita Falls on U.S. 281. After 6.8 miles turn left (east) on RR 1954 and follow it 7.2 miles to Lake Arrowhead State Park. Then, make your way to Seymour, Texas, by heading west through Archer City. Find Seymour City Park south and east of the intersection of U.S. 183 and U.S. 82 in Seymour. If you have made prior arrangements for access, continue about 18 miles west to the privately owned Ranger Creek Ranch (access can be obtained by contacts at www.RangerCreekRanch.com) to explore mesas and canyons.

Habitats: Mesquite brush, rolling prairie, open water, rivers

Try to find: In Lake Arrowhead State Park, scissor-tailed flycatcher, western kingbird. northern bobwhite, wild turkey, burrowing owls, Forster's tern, least tern, and Neotropic cormorant; in Lucy Park, Mississippi kites, Carolina wren, Carolina chickadee, mourning dove, Inca dove, snowy egret, killdeer, and migrating songbirds during spring and fall; in Seymour City Park, wild turkey, killdeer, Mississippi kites, and black-bellied whistling ducks

29 Fort Hood (Killeen)

Why: An unusual place to find unique birds, the largest U.S. Army base in the country hosts two species of conservation concern and protects a variety of habitats in concert with The Nature Conservancy and the U.S. Fish and Wildlife Service.

64. The black-capped vireo is one species of conservation concern that is protected on the grounds of Fort Hood, Texas. Photo of individual with leg bands used for critical research is by Gil Eckrich, USFWS volunteer.

Habitats: Oak/juniper woodlands and savannahs

Try to find: Two protected species nest on the site: golden-cheeked warbler and black-capped vireo; other breeding birds include white-eyed vireo, Carolina chickadee, blue-gray gnatcatcher, Mississippi kite, black-capped vireo, ash-throated flycatcher, Bell's vireo, Bewick's wren, and black-crested titmouse

Special instructions: To gain access to this controlled facility involves several steps: (1) visit the Fort Hood Visitors Center to request access to Fort Hood; (2) at the visitors center provide the following information (unless you already have a valid Department of Defense ID card): the reason for entering the installation, a valid driver's license, current vehicle registration and proof of insurance (for driver), license plate number, and the destination within Fort Hood, name of facility, building number, street address, or unit name/designation; (3) go to the sportsman center to complete a release form and pay an access fee for birding or hunting/fishing. A topographic map will be provided, and visitors with access can then use an online system to search for army training areas that are open for birding (or hunting/fishing). A birder can sign into a maximum of three training areas. Visitors must sign out by the end of the day, and following directions is critical to avoid penalties. Visitors much pay attention for tanks or heavy equipment, and care must be taken to only enter areas for which you have permission and to not enter areas coded red on the map that have live fire.

30 Hagarman National Wildlife Refuge (west of Pottsboro)

Why: This is a great spot to see migrating birds and wintering waterfowl in large flocks. The local bird list is just short of 350 species.

Habitats: Open water, shallow water, mudflats, woodland, grassland

Try to find: In winter, greater white-fronted geese, snow geese, Ross's geese, cackling geese, Canada geese, bald eagle; in fall, roseate spoonbill; during breeding season, wood duck, northern bobwhite, wild turkey, pied-billed grebe, Neotropic cormorant, tricolored heron, Mississippi kite, common gallinule, black-necked stilt, least tern, greater roadrunner, scissor-tailed flycatcher, loggerhead shrike, prothonotary warbler, grasshopper sparrow, painted bunting, and dickcissel

31 Dogwood Canyon Audubon Center (near downtown Dallas in Cedar Hill)

Why: This forest of over two hundred acres is known for rare species in a zone where species from east, west, and central Texas converge.

Habitats: An urban greenbelt area composed of forested canyon, grassland, and open water

Try to find: Painted bunting, summer tanager, golden-crowned kinglet, brown creeper, red-shouldered hawk, hermit thrush, black-chinned hummingbird, white-eyed vireo, red-eyed vireo, warbling vireo, red-bellied woodpecker, downy woodpecker, Chuck-will's-widow, blue-gray gnatcatcher

32 Lost Maples State Natural Area (north of Vanderpool)

Why: Don't miss this beautiful area in the Texas hill country. A visit here can be combined with a stop at the South Llano River State Park, less than an hour to the south.

Habitats: Bigtooth maple forest, river canyons

Try to find: Black-capped vireo, golden-cheeked warbler, wild turkey, greater roadrunner, ruby-throated hummingbird, black-chinned hummingbird, green kingfisher, ash-throated flycatcher, yellow-throated vireo, Hutton's vireo, western scrub-jay, black-crested titmouse, Louisiana waterthrush, rufous-crowned sparrow, painted bunting, Scott's oriole, and lesser goldfinch

33 Balcones Canyonlands National Wildlife Refuge (south of Oatmeal)

Why: Seven miles of trails with overlooks and photo blinds help you enjoy old-growth cedar forests, meadows, shrublands, and rocky creeks in hill country. See if you encounter one of the introduced and feral emus present throughout the year.

Habitats: Shinnery oak thickets, juniper, grasslands, spring-fed creek

Try to find: Black-capped vireo, northern mockingbird, white-eyed vireo, rufous-crowned sparrow, yellow-breasted chat, painted bunting, northern bobwhite, Bewick's wren, northern cardinal, rufous-crowned sparrow, field sparrow, golden-cheeked warbler, black-and-white warblers; in winter, spotted towhees

65. American avocets (*center*) and blue-winged teal in a shallow wetland. Photo by Ethan Freese.

SUGGESTED RESOURCES

The Audubon Bird Guide. Over 800 species. Photos. Range maps. Allows upload of photo for other users to see. Bird id feature can guide you to potential species from your description of what you saw. Audio clips. Sightings feature allows you to keep record of your bird list. Connect real-time to eBird to see what other birders are reporting near you. News on conservation and science from Audubon. (Free)

iBird Pro Guide to Birds: Field Guide to North America. 946 species. Illustrations and photos. Range maps. Details on appearance, habitat, behavior, conservation, size, weight, color pattern, sexual differences. In-app purchases allow addition of birds from other countries. Time of Day feature allows searches by activity level. Birds Around Me feature can show only species at your location. Splits-History allows you to follow name changes as birds are split into two species or lumped into one over time. No internet connection needed during use. (Fee)

Merlin Bird ID by Cornell Lab. Over 2,000 species. High-quality photos. Range maps. Allows upload of photo for matching to obtain ID. Alternatively, answer five questions about the bird you see to get a short list of potential matches. Customized lists of birds for time of year near you from the eBird citizen science database. Audio recordings. Can work without internet connection if you plan ahead and store your destination information. (Free)

The Sibley eGuide to the Birds of North America. 810 species. Illustrations perched and in-flight, above and below. Range maps. Personal sighting log. Filter species to single state or province or

to only common birds. Catalog of variation of calls and songs
by region. Filter by color, shape, size, and habits. Compare two
species on the same screen. Song Sleuth can help identify songs
of 200 common birds. No internet connection needed during
use. (Fee)

BOOKS/PUBLICATIONS

Birds of the Great Plains. Bob Jennings, Ted Cable, and Roger Burrows
(Auburn WA: Lone Pine, 2005).A description of 325 species of
birds in the plains and their habitat for nesting, their diet, and
their songs and calls, as well as recommendations of places to
visit to see birds.

Birds of the Great Plains: Breeding Species and Their Distribution. Paul
Johnsgard (Lincoln: University of Nebraska Press, 1979). A 420-
page volume that serves as the first attempt to catalog all bird
species known to have bred in the Great Plains.

*Birds of the Untamed West: The History of Birdlife in Nebraska, 1750–
1875*. James E. Ducey (Omaha ne: Making History, 2000). A
detailed set of notes of references to birds from a period with
little documentation in the main literature. Discover uses of
birds by Indians on the plains and follow explorers and early
naturalists as they start to document the diversity of bird life in
the region.

"Fossil Birds of the Nebraska Region." James E. Ducey (*Transactions of
the Nebraska Academy of Sciences* 19 (1992): 83–96). An intrigu-
ing look back at fossil evidence through various time periods.
Published in Volume 130 of the Transactions of the Nebraska
Academy of Sciences and Affiliated Societies.

Great Wildlife of the Great Plains. Paul Johnsgard (Lawrence: University Press of Kansas, 2003). An overview of wildlife, including
birds, in the plains that is useful for residents or visitors.

Prairie Birds: Fragile Splendor in the Great Plains. Paul Johnsgard
(Lawrence: University Press of Kansas, 2001). The life history
and associated stories of thirty-three select species of birds living
on the plains.

The Sibley Guide to Bird Life and Behavior. David Sibley (New York:
Knopf, flexibound edition, 2009). A comprehensive guide to the

things birds do that make them interesting. A must-have if you want to understand the birds you view.

Wings over the Great Plains: Bird Migrations in the Central Flyway. Paul Johnsgard (Lincoln N E: Zea Books, 2012). A thorough description of 400 species of birds on the Great Plains and 140 localities important to migration and from which to view birds.

WEBSITES

eBird. Cornell Lab of Ornithology. A citizen science project that allows you to keep track of your bird lists, photos, and sounds while you explore the latest sightings from around the world. http://ebird.org/.

Birding in the United States. National Audubon Society. An interactive state-by-state guide to birding hotspots. https://www.audubon.org/travel.

Birds of Nebraska Online. Nebraska Game and Parks Commission. Detailed species accounts of Nebraska birds. http://www.birdsofnebraska.org.

Montana Field Guide: Birds. Montana Fish, Wildlife, and Parks. Links to species accounts of Montana birds. http://fieldguide.mt.gov/displayFamily.aspx?class=Aves.

South Dakota Birds, Birding and Nature. Private individual. Birding hotspots, identification tips and quizzes, and photos. https://www.sdakotabirds.com/.

The Top 50 Ecotourism Sites in the Great Plains. Great Plains Ecotourism Coalition, Center for Great Plains Studies, University of Nebraska–Lincoln. An annotated, interactive map of some of the best destinations for ecotourists (including birders) in the Great Plains. https://visittheprairie.com/route/.

Wyoming Birds. Wyoming Game and Fish Department. Links to informative species accounts for nongame birds of conservation concern. https://wgfd.wyo.gov/Habitat/Habitat-Plans/Wyoming-State-Wildlife-Action-Plan/Birds-(1).

Page numbers in italic indicate illustrations.

geese: brant, 97; Canada goose, 12; images of, *57*; impacts of agriculture on, 76; impacts of climate change on, 118; market hunting of, 104; migration of, 52, 144; reflex behaviors of, 27; snow goose, 2, 54, 56, *57*, 76

glaciations, 39, 44, 54, 61, 63

golden eagles, 2, *3*, 103

goldfinches, *119*

gold rush, 94–95, 112

grasshopper sparrows, 41; images of, *7*; impact of climate change on, *119*; as near-endemic species, 43; population declines, 71; vocalizations of, 9

grasslands: bird watching in, 142–44; formation of, 39, 40; habitat loss in, 71; impact of agriculture on, 30, 40–41; impact of climate change on, 124; impact on speciation, 61; management strategies, 124; as a simple system, 41–44. *See also* Great Plains; habitat

gray partridges (introduced species), 115, *119*

great blue herons, *119*

Great Depression, 73–74, 130–32

greater prairie-chickens: distribution of, 1; habitat of, 47–49; honored by Native Americans, 88; hunting of, 99; images of, *21*, *48*; mating behaviors of, 20–23, 88; as near-endemic species, 43

greater sage-grouse, 76–77, *78*, 93

great grey owls, 149

great-horned owls, *119*, 146

Great Plains: climate of, 53–54; common birds of, 2–14; endemic species of, 41–50; as "flyover country," 29–30; geologic history of, 30–31, 33, 35–41, 60–63, 117; impact of climate change on, 116–25; land cover, *31*; west-to-east rivers of, 36–37, 39

grebes: images of, *19*; mating behaviors of, 18–20; pied-billed grebe, 35, *119*; western grebe, 18–20

green-winged teal, 35, *119*

Grinnell, Joseph, 113

Griswold, Samuel, 105

ground nests, 25–28

grouse: distribution of, 1; fossil records of, 35; greater sage-grouse, 76–77, *78*, 93; images of, *24*, *164*; impact of climate change on, *119*; impacts of agriculture on, 76–77; mating behaviors, 22–25, 76; precocial chicks of, 6; sharp-tailed grouse, 1, 22–25, 43, 99, *119*, 148, *164*; species of, 49. *See also* prairie-chickens (grouse)

Grudzien, T. A., *62*

Guide to the Kansas Pacific Railway (Weston), 99–100

Gypsum Hills Wildlife Drive (KS), 170–71

IN THE DISCOVER THE GREAT PLAINS SERIES

Great Plains Weather
Kenneth F. Dewey

Great Plains Geology
R. F. Diffendal Jr.

Great Plains Politics
Peter J. Longo

Great Plains Bison
Dan O'Brien

Great Plains Birds
Larkin Powell

Great Plains Literature
Linda Ray Pratt

Great Plains Indians
David J. Wishart

Discover the Great Plains, a series from the Center for Great
Plains Studies and the University of Nebraska Press, offers concise
introductions to the natural wonders, diverse cultures, history,
and contemporary life of the Great Plains. To order or obtain
more information on these or other University of Nebraska Press
titles, visit nebraskapress.unl.edu.